Stock Market Starter: A Beginner's Guide to Investing

Building Wealth One Share at a Time

Lucas Thompson

Table of Contents

INTRODUCTION

This is "Stock Market Starter: A Beginner's Guide to Investing: Building Wealth One Share at a Time." This book serves as your entryway into the fascinating investing world, giving you the knowledge and self-assurance you need to begin trading stocks. This guide is designed to satisfy your goals, whether your goal is to prepare for retirement, accumulate long-term wealth, or learn the basics of the market.

You will find key ideas, valuable tactics, and necessary resources in the following sections to assist you in making wise investing choices. We'll demystify market habits, explain intricate financial terms, and provide step-by-step directions on opening your first brokerage account, evaluating equities, and assembling a diverse portfolio.

At first, investing may seem overwhelming, but it can be a profitable and powerful activity with the correct advice. You will have a strong foundation in stock market trading and the self-assurance to increase your money, one share at a time, by the time you finish reading this book. Together, let's take this trip to realize the full potential of your financial future.

CHAPTER I

The Basics of the Stock Market

What is a Stock?

Stocks, also known as shares or equity, are interests in a company that reflect ownership. These ownership rights are bought and sold on stock exchanges, such as the New York Stock swap (NYSE) or NASDAQ. On these exchanges, individuals or institutions purchase stocks, which represent a share of the assets and profits of the company. This process of buying and selling stocks is how ownership of publicly traded corporations is transferred.

Equities play a part in corporate ownership is one of their core characteristics. Businesses issue stocks to raise money for operations, expansion projects, R&D, or other strategic activities. Companies raise money by selling investors stocks, which they may use to support expansion prospects debt-free. Investors who buy stocks in exchange for a portion of the company's income in the form of dividends and voting rights over corporate decisions become shareholders.

The market dynamics of supply and demand impact a stock's price. A number of factors, including investor attitude, industry trends, corporate performance, and geopolitical events, influence stock prices. A stock's price usually increases when demand outpaces supply, indicating investor confidence in the company's future. On the other hand, if supply outpaces demand, the stock price can drop as a result of worries or unfavourable sentiment among investors.

Investors purchase stocks for various reasons, but primarily to increase the value of their investments. Capital appreciation is one method by which stock investments can benefit investors. Investors may realize a capital gain when they sell their shares at a more excellent price than when they first purchased them if the cost of the stock rises over time. Capital appreciation is a crucial tactic for long-term investors looking to accumulate wealth through investments in businesses with robust growth prospects and a competitive edge in their respective sectors.

Dividends are just another way that stocks are advantageous to investors. Distributions of a company's profits to shareholders, known as dividends, are often made quarterly or yearly. Only some businesses pay dividends, and the size of payouts varies according to management choices and profitability. Income-oriented investors looking for steady income streams and the possibility of dividend increases over time are drawn to dividend-paying equities.

Various stocks are distinguished by firm size, growth potential, and investing attributes. Common stock is the most common kind, which entitles the owner to vote rights and the possibility of dividend payments. Conversely, preferred stock may not have voting rights but usually pays fixed dividends. Value stocks are cheap in relation to their inherent value and might present appealing prospects for long-term investors; growth stocks are shares of companies predicted to grow at an above-average rate compared to the broader market.

Hazards associated with stock investing include company-specific hazards, market volatility, economic downturns, and geopolitical events that could affect stock prices. Spreading assets over various equities and asset classes, or diversification, is crucial to reduce risks and improve overall portfolio stability. Investors can lessen the impact of unfavourable occurrences on certain stocks or sectors while seizing growth opportunities across a range of market segments by diversifying their holdings.

Due to their ability to facilitate wealth creation, liquidity availability, and capital allocation, stock markets are essential to the global economy. Investors engage in the stock market to profit from corporate profitability and economic growth, as well as to deploy capital effectively and invest in innovative enterprises. To maintain fair and orderly stock trading, stock exchanges offer transparency, price discovery tools, and regulatory control. This promotes investor confidence and market integrity.

In summary, stocks offer investors chances for portfolio diversification, dividend income, and capital growth as they reflect ownership in businesses exchanged on stock exchanges. Investors can better navigate the complexity of equity investing by understanding the basics of stocks, including their position in company ownership, variables influencing stock prices, investment methods, types of stocks, risks, and advantages. Stocks are a fundamental component of long-term wealth-building and financial planning methods since they present potential benefits and inherent dangers, regardless of whether one is investing for growth, income, or both.

How Stocks Are Traded

Understanding the complex procedures and systems that investors use to purchase and sell ownership stakes in publicly traded companies on stock exchanges across the globe is essential to understanding how stocks are traded. This process is essential to capital allocation, investor engagement, and global economic activity. It is made possible by contemporary financial markets.

Typically, stock trading occurs on regulated exchanges like the London Stock Exchange, NASDAQ, and the New York Stock Exchange (NYSE). These exchanges offer centralized venues for executing trades between buyers and sellers. Investors place orders via online trading platforms or brokerage houses to start trading. Orders fall into various categories based on how they are to be executed. These include market orders, limit orders, and stop orders, all intended to achieve particular trading goals.

One of the simplest kinds of orders is a market order, which directs brokers to purchase or sell a stock at the going rate in the market. These orders are filled quickly and at the best price offered during the order. Market orders, frequently utilized when trading highly liquid stocks with narrow bid-ask spreads, are appropriate for investors looking for instant trade execution.

Alternatively, limit orders let investors designate a minimum or maximum price to sell or purchase a stock. Investors have control over the price at which their orders are executed because they are only cancelled once the predetermined price conditions are satisfied. Investors could get better execution prices and prevent unfavourable price volatility by using limit orders, which offer flexibility and price control.

Stop orders restrict possible losses or lock in profits at predefined price levels. They include stop-loss and stop-limit orders. To help investors limit losses during market declines or unfavourable price movements, a stop-loss order automatically initiates a market sell order when a stock's price drops to a specified level. By defining a price range within which an order should be executed once a stop price is reached, stop-limit orders combine the advantages of limit and stop orders. This gives traders more control over trade execution and reduces price volatility.

Once orders are sent to brokerage firms or trading platforms, they are routed to stock exchanges, where they join the order book. The order book, maintained by exchanges, displays real-time information about buy and sell orders for each stock, including price levels and order quantities. The continuous matching of buy and sell orders determines stock prices and facilitates efficient price discovery in the market.

Stock exchanges operate using electronic trading systems that match buy and sell orders based on price-time priority. A trade happens when a buy order and a sell order game at a particular price, and the transaction is instantly recorded. By enforcing rules and regulations governing order execution, market manipulation, and insider trading, exchanges ensure transparency and fairness in trading, maintaining investor confidence and market integrity.

Stocks can be traded over-the-counter (OTC) through decentralized broker-dealer networks and organized exchanges. OTC trading, which often involves smaller businesses or securities not listed on major exchanges, is direct trading between buyers and sellers. OTC markets provide liquidity and accessibility for trading stocks that may not meet formal exchanges' listing requirements, offering investors alternative investment opportunities.

The role of market makers is crucial in facilitating trading activities on both exchanges and OTC markets. Market makers are financial firms or individuals that provide liquidity by quoting bids and asking prices for specific stocks. They stand ready to buy or sell securities at publicly quoted prices, ensuring continuous trading and narrow bid-ask spreads. Market makers play a vital role in price stabilization, efficient market functioning, and liquidity provision, benefiting investors by enhancing market efficiency and reducing transaction costs.

Various factors influence stock trading, including market dynamics, economic conditions, company news, geopolitical events, investor sentiment, and regulatory developments. These factors contribute to stock price volatility and trading volumes, influencing investor behavior and market trends. Investors routinely use technical and fundamental analysis to evaluate companies, find trading opportunities, and make informed decisions based on price patterns, market trends, financial data, and company performance.

In conclusion, stock trading is a dynamic process that facilitates the buying and selling ownership stakes in publicly traded companies on organized exchanges and over-the-counter markets. Understanding how stocks are traded involves knowledge of order types, market mechanics, trading strategies, and the role of market participants such as investors, brokerage firms, exchanges, and market makers. By mastering the complexity of stock trading, investors can capitalize on investment opportunities, manage risk, and achieve their financial objectives in a global marketplace driven by innovation, efficiency, and continual market change.

Key Stock Market Terms

Understanding key stock market terms is essential for anyone looking to navigate the complexities of investing in equities. These words are the cornerstone of financial literacy, empowering investors to evaluate market circumstances, make well-informed judgments, and create profitable trading plans. A solid understanding of these concepts is essential for effective investment, ranging from fundamental ideas like stocks and bonds to more complex words like P/E ratios, market capitalization, and beyond.

The idea of a stock, which stands for ownership in a corporation, is fundamental to the stock market. An individual who buys stock acquires a share in the business, making them entitled to a percentage of its assets and earnings. There are two types of stocks: common stock and preferred stock. In addition to voting on corporate decisions, common stockholders are also eligible to receive dividends, which are payouts of the company's profits. Although preferred investors sometimes receive regular dividends and have a higher claim on assets and revenues, they usually do not have voting rights.

A corporation pays its shareholders dividends, usually deducted from profits. These may be given out as more stock shares or cash. A financial statistic called the dividend yield illustrates how much a corporation pays out in dividends annually in relation to the price of its stock. It is computed by dividing the price per share of the company by the annual dividends per share. A greater dividend yield suggests that the investment may produce an income stream that is more alluring.

The total value of a company's outstanding shares of stock is its market capitalization, also sometimes known as its market cap. The current share price multiplied by the total number of outstanding shares is how it is computed. Large-cap, mid-cap, and small-cap stocks are examples of market cap classifications; these stocks reflect businesses with varying sizes and market values. Small-cap stocks are frequently newer businesses with more significant development potential but also higher risk, whereas large-cap stocks are usually well-established enterprises with reliable earnings.

A crucial measure of a business's profitability is earnings per share (EPS), which is determined by dividing net income by the total number of outstanding shares. It is a measure of a company's financial health since it shows how much of its earnings are allotted to each exceptional share of common stock. A higher EPS indicates greater profitability. Another critical number that indicates how much investors are ready to pay for every dollar of earnings is the price-to-earnings (P/E) ratio. By dividing the current stock price by the EPS, it is computed. A stock may be overpriced if its P/E ratio is high and undervalued if it has a low P/E ratio.

Exchanges, which are online marketplaces for buying and selling stocks and other assets, constitute the backbone of the stock market. The New York Stock Exchange (NYSE) and Nasdaq are significant exchanges. When new securities are issued and sold to investors for the first time, like in an IPO, they do so on the primary market. Conversely, existing securities are traded among investors on the secondary market. Most individuals are familiar with this market, where equities are exchanged for one another.

The general stock price trend can be considered bull or bear. Rising stock prices and optimistic investor sentiment, frequently propelled by positive economic indicators and business profits, are hallmarks of a bull market. On the other hand, a bear market, usually brought on by a downturn in the economy or poor company performance, is characterized by falling stock prices and generalized pessimism. Investors can better match their tactics to the current market conditions by thoroughly understanding these market trends.

The ease with which an asset can be purchased or sold on the market without depressing its price is referred to as liquidity. Because they are traded in larger volumes, the stocks of more established, larger corporations are typically more liquid. On the other hand, smaller companies' equities could be less liquid. Liquidity is significant because it influences the speed and price at which an investor can enter or exit a position.

When a business issues extra shares in order to reduce the price per share and make the stock more accessible to a broader group of investors, this is known as a stock split. For instance, in a 2-for-1 stock split, the price per share is cut in half, and each existing share is split into two. The overall value of an investor's shares stays constant even if the number of shares grows. The converse is called a reverse stock split, in which a business decreases the number of outstanding shares to raise the price per share.

The fluctuation in a stock's price over time is measured by its volatility. A stock with high volatility can see significant price swings quickly, whereas a stock with low volatility would see more steady pricing. A standard risk indicator is volatility; greater volatility implies higher risk and more significant profits.

The index, a statistical indicator of a set of stocks' performance, is another crucial concept. The S&P 500, Dow Jones Industrial Average (DJIA), and Nasdaq Composite are three essential stock indices. These indexes monitor the performance of particular equities and serve as a standard for the market or specific industry segments. Investors use indexes to assess market performance, evaluate portfolio performance, and make well-informed investment decisions.

A stock's volatility about the whole market is gauged by its beta. A stock's price that moves in tandem with the market is said to have a beta of 1. More volatility than the market is indicated by a beta greater than 1, while lesser volatility is indicated by a beta less than 1. Investors can better grasp a stock's market risk and potential impact on their portfolios by looking at beta.

Two essential ideas in stock trading are market orders and limit orders. A market order is an order to purchase or sell stock at the best price right away. It promises performance but not cost. A limit order, on the other hand, establishes the highest or lowest price at which an investor is prepared to purchase or sell. Because the stock must reach the designated price for the trade, this kind of order guarantees the price but not the execution.

Selling stock that you borrowed to repurchase it at a cheaper price later is known as short selling. Investors who believe the stock price will drop employ this tactic if the stock price drops, the investor keeps the difference after purchasing the shares at a reduced cost and returning them to the lender. Since there is a theoretically infinite chance of loss if the stock price rises rather than falls, short selling entails a high level of risk.

Buying shares through margin trading entails borrowing funds from a broker. This raises the possibility of losses while boosting the possible returns for investors by enabling them to purchase more shares than they could with their current finances. The amount borrowed is referred to as the margin, and to protect against possible losses, the investor's account needs to keep a minimum balance or maintenance margin.

For dividend investors, knowing the ex-dividend date is essential. The cutoff date on which a stock starts trading without the value of its upcoming dividend payment is known as the ex-dividend date. Investors must own the shares before the ex-dividend date to be eligible for the dividend. New stock purchasers will not be eligible to receive the impending dividend on or after this date.

The difference between the greatest price a buyer is ready to pay (the bid) and the lowest price a seller is willing to take (the ask) is known as the bid-ask spread. A more significant gap suggests less liquidity and possibly higher trading costs for investors, a narrower spread denotes a more liquid market with higher trade activity.

The value of a company's assets, as shown on its balance sheet, less its obligations, is represented by a stock's book value. It estimates the company's value in the event of a liquidation and full repayment of all debts. The company's total book value is divided by the number of outstanding shares to get the book value per share. Investors can determine if a stock is overvalued or undervalued by comparing the market price to book value.

In technical analysis, future stock movements are predicted by examining price charts and trade volume. Moving averages, which smooth out price data to reveal trends, and the relative strength index (RSI), which gauges the rate and variance of price moves to pinpoint overbought or oversold situations, are essential instruments in technical analysis. Technical analysts use these and other indicators to make trading decisions based on past price patterns.

In contrast, fundamental analysis concentrates on assessing a company's competitive position, growth potential, financial stability, and quality of management. Revenue, net income, profit margins, return on equity (ROE), and debt-to-equity ratio are essential metrics in fundamental analysis. Investors seek to ascertain a stock's intrinsic worth and evaluate its prospects for long-term growth by examining these variables.

In summary, mastering the stock market jargon is crucial to navigating the intricate world of investing. Financial literacy is based on terms like stocks, dividends, market capitalization, earnings per share, P/E ratio, liquidity, volatility, and indexes. Furthermore, ideas like limit orders, market orders, margin trading, short selling, and technical and fundamental research give investors the power to control risk, make well-informed decisions, and create winning investment plans. By learning these concepts, investors can better grasp market dynamics, spot opportunities, and reach their financial objectives.

CHAPTER II

Getting Started with Investing

Setting Your Financial Goals

Achieving financial success and security requires setting financial goals. Whether your financial objectives are paying for college, buying a home, preparing for retirement, or just maintaining a comfortable lifestyle, having specific, well-defined financial goals gives you focus and drive. This essay examines the value of establishing financial objectives, how to define them, and practical methods for reaching them.

Financial goals are crucial because they act as a road map for your financial journey. Making wise judgments regarding spending, investing, and saving is easier when you have clear goals. Setting goals gives your financial actions a feeling of direction and purpose, making allocating resources easier. They also provide a standard by which you can evaluate your development, allowing you to stay on course and make the required corrections.

Evaluating your existing financial status is the first step toward creating financial goals. This entails assessing your earnings, outlays, investments, debts, and savings. Knowing where you stand financially serves as a basis for establishing reasonable and doable objectives. Making a thorough budget that breaks down your monthly income and expenses is crucial since it will show you where to make savings and cost reductions.

You can start setting your financial goals as soon as you have a firm understanding of your financial condition. These objectives must be time-bound, meaningful, quantifiable, achievable, and targeted (SMART). There are precise, well-defined objectives, like setting up $20,000 for a down payment on a home. Measurable objectives, like saving $500 monthly, let you monitor your progress. In light of your existing financial circumstances, attainable goals are reasonable and doable. Relevant goals complement your beliefs and overarching financial goals. Time-bound objectives provide you with a sense of urgency and drive since they have a set deadline.

There are three types of financial goals: short-term, medium-term, and long-term. One year is the time frame for achieving short-term goals like emergency fund building or debt repayment from high-interest credit cards. One to five years is the average duration of medium-term goals, including supporting college, going on vacation, or saving for a car. Long-term objectives go beyond five years, including crucial financial turning points such as purchasing a home, setting aside money for retirement, or leaving a legacy for your loved ones.

Creating an emergency reserve is a crucial short-term financial objective. A savings account used as a buffer against unforeseen costs, including auto repairs, medical problems, or job loss, is known as an emergency fund. A readily accessible account should be used to save three to six months' worth of living expenditures, according to financial experts. Your capacity to pay unexpected expenses with high-interest debt is prevented when you have an emergency fund, which safeguards your ability to maintain a stable economic situation.

Another essential short-term objective is debt repayment. Credit card debt, which has a high interest rate, has the potential to rapidly balloon out of control, causing financial strain and restricting your capacity to save and make investments. Making debt repayment a priority, starting with the loans with the highest interest rates, might lessen your financial load and free up funds for other objectives. Debt management techniques such as the avalanche method, which targets high-interest loans, and the snowball method, which concentrates on paying off the lowest bills first, can be successful.

Planning is necessary for medium-term financial goals since they frequently involve essential life events. For instance, saving for a down payment on a house usually means putting aside a sizeable sum of money spread over several years. It's critical to do your homework on the housing market, comprehend the costs of homeownership, and establish a savings strategy that fits into your spending plan. Similarly, financing your or your children's education requires knowing how much tuition will cost, what financial aid alternatives are available, and setting up a specific education savings account, such as a 529 plan.

Long-term financial objectives, like retirement planning, call for proactive planning and careful saving and investing. Estimating your future living needs, comprehending social security payments, and optimizing contributions to retirement accounts such as 401(k)s or IRAs are all part of retirement planning. For your investments to grow tremendously, thanks to compound interest, you must begin saving for retirement as soon as possible. Staying on course to reach your retirement goals is ensured by routinely assessing and modifying your plan.

A crucial element of reaching long-term financial objectives is investing. Although a standard bank account provides minimal growth potential because of its low interest rate, saving money in one is safe. Higher returns can be obtained by investing in stocks, bonds, mutual funds, or real estate, but hazards are also involved. Investing in a diverse range of asset types can help you reduce risk and maximize your potential for gain. Developing an investing plan that fits your financial objectives and risk tolerance can be significantly aided by working with a financial advisor.

It's critical to assess and modify your financial strategies and goals periodically. Your economic condition may vary due to life circumstances, such as changes in your family's size, income, or health, and your goals may need to be adjusted. Keeping a close eye on your savings, investments, and budget will help you remain on course and make wise choices. Setting goals and acknowledging accomplishments can also inspire and support responsible financial practices.

Setting and accomplishing financial objectives are significantly aided by financial literacy. Knowing the fundamentals of money management, including budgeting, investing, saving, and credit management, can enable you to make wise choices and steer clear of frequent traps. Your financial literacy can be improved by utilizing various tools, such as books, online courses, and workshops on financial planning. Consulting with economic experts, like advisors or planners, can offer tailored direction and assistance.

When setting financial goals, you should also consider your legacy and long-term financial security. Estate planning, which involves naming beneficiaries, establishing trusts, and writing a will, guarantees that your assets are allocated in a way that best serves your family. Another crucial component of financial planning is life insurance, which provides your family with financial security in the case of your passing. You may build a thorough monetary strategy that offers you and your family security and peace of mind by considering these factors.

Financial planning should be considered as a family in addition to individual financial objectives. Maintaining open lines of communication among family members regarding budgeting, savings targets, and financial priorities ensures that everyone is on the same page and working toward the same goals. Early financial education establishes sound financial habits in kids and prepares them for future financial independence. Financial planning for families also involves discussing and preparing for significant life events like retirement, college costs, and weddings.

Achieving financial well-being and peace of mind is just as important as building wealth regarding financial goals. Being in control of your daily money, being able to withstand financial setbacks, staying on course to reach your financial objectives, and having the financial flexibility to make decisions that let you enjoy life are all parts of being financially well-off. A balanced approach to money management that prioritizes saving and spending in a way consistent with your beliefs and life goals is necessary to achieve financial well-being.

Creating financial goals is critical to reaching financial success and stability. You can make a financial roadmap by evaluating your financial status, setting SMART goals, and grouping them into short-, medium--, and long-term targets. Important milestones in this process include setting up an emergency fund, paying off debt, saving for significant life events, and making retirement plans. Practical financial goal setting includes regular goal reviews and adjustments, improving your financial literacy, and taking family planning and long-term financial security into account. To achieve financial well-being and peace of mind, it is ultimately necessary to practice discipline, make wise decisions, and manage your money sensibly.

Building Your Investment Portfolio

Building an investment portfolio is a critical endeavor for anyone seeking to achieve long-term financial goals and ensure financial security. In addition to aiding in wealth accumulation, a well-built portfolio also aids in risk management when investing. Understanding investment concepts, establishing goals, determining risk tolerance, diversifying investments, and continuing management and evaluation are all steps in the process of creating an investment portfolio. This essay explores these areas in depth to offer a thorough how-to manual for creating a successful investing portfolio.

Gaining an understanding of the fundamentals of investing is the first step towards constructing an investment portfolio. Investing is the process of placing money with the goal of making a profit over time in financial assets including stocks, bonds, mutual funds, real estate, and other vehicles. The main objective is to increase wealth while controlling the dangers involved. Understanding risk and return is essential since they are intertwined in the investing process. As larger potential returns are often accompanied by higher risks, creating a successful portfolio requires striking a balance between the two.

Establishing precise financial goals is the first stage in creating an investment portfolio. These goals ought to line up with your time horizon, risk tolerance, and overall financial ambitions. For example, if you are saving for a thirty-year-off retirement, you may be more tolerant of increased volatility in exchange for long-term growth. On the other hand, you might favor assets with lower risk and more consistent returns if you are saving for a short-term objective, such a down payment on a home within the next five years. Creating a targeted investment strategy is aided by the establishment of SMART (specific, measurable, achievable, relevant, and time-bound objectives.

Risk tolerance is a critical factor in portfolio construction. It speaks to the extent of return variability on investments that a person is prepared to bear. Age, income, financial situation, and investment knowledge are factors that affect one's ability to tolerate risk. Because they have more time to recuperate from potential losses, younger investors usually have a higher risk tolerance. On the other hand, older investors who are getting close to retirement could favor safer assets in order to protect their cash. Determining the right asset allocation for your portfolio involves evaluating your risk tolerance.

The process of distributing an investment portfolio among several asset classes, such as stocks, bonds, real estate, and cash, is known as asset allocation. Optimizing the portfolio's risk-return profile is the aim of asset allocation. Different asset classes tend to perform differently over time and have unique risk and return characteristics. You can lower the portfolio's overall risk by spreading your assets among a variety of asset classes. Bonds, for instance, may offer stability when equities do poorly, and vice versa. An asset mix found in a well-balanced portfolio usually corresponds to your investing objectives and risk tolerance.

 Stocks, or equities, represent ownership in a company and offer the potential for high returns through capital appreciation and dividends. Although they are typically seen as riskier than other asset types, they have the potential to expand significantly over time. Bonds, often known as fixed-income instruments, are loans given to governments or businesses that are repaid with principal at maturity and recurring interest payments. They are good for conservative investors since they are usually less volatile than equities and offer a consistent income stream. Investing in real estate can profit from diversity as well as the possibility of gain and income from rental properties. Although they often give lesser returns, cash and cash equivalents—such as money market funds and savings accounts—provide stability and liquidity.

When constructing an investment portfolio, diversification is an essential tactic. To lower risk, it entails distributing investments over a range of asset classes, industries, regions, and securities. The theory behind this is that a diverse portfolio can offset the bad performance of some investments with the superior performance of others, therefore making large losses less likely. Investing in mutual funds or exchange-traded funds (ETFs), which offer exposure to a wide range of securities inside a single investment, is one way to achieve diversification. Other strategies can also be used. Furthermore, taking into account both local and foreign investments can increase diversification and lower exposure to hazards unique to a given nation.

A thorough investigation and analysis are necessary when choosing individual investments. A company's competitive position, growth potential, financial health, and valuation should all be considered while selecting stocks. In order to evaluate a company's profitability, debt levels, and general financial health, fundamental analysis entails looking over financial statements like income statements, balance sheets, and cash flow statements. To forecast future price changes, technical analysis, on the other hand, focuses on past price patterns and trading volumes.

For the purpose of making wise financial decisions, both strategies can offer insightful information. Bond selection should be based on maturity dates, interest rates, and credit quality. A bond's credit rating indicates its capacity to pay back principal and interest; higher-rated bonds are often safer but have lower yields. Bond prices are inversely correlated with interest rates; when rates rise, bond prices decrease, and vice versa. The principal will be returned on the maturity date; longer-term bonds generally have higher yields but more interest rate risk. Building a bond portfolio that satisfies your risk tolerance and income requirements requires striking a balance between these variables.

When making real estate investments, one must take into account the property's nature, location, market trends, and potential for gain and income. Purchasing and managing real estate can result in a reliable source of income as well as the possibility of capital gains when investing directly in rental properties. With the help of real estate investment trusts (REITs), investors can access real estate without having to deal with the hassles of property management. In addition to investing in a diverse portfolio of real estate assets and being traded like stocks, REITs also offer the advantages of liquidity and diversification.

Maintaining a consistent level of alignment between your investing strategy and your risk tolerance and goals requires ongoing portfolio maintenance and evaluation. It is easier to spot deviations from your original plan and make the required adjustments when you keep a regular eye on the performance of your investments. A crucial component of managing a portfolio is rebalancing, which is modifying the asset allocation on a regular basis to keep the intended level of risk. For example, you might need to sell some assets and reinvest in failing ones to bring the portfolio back into balance if a certain asset class performs better than expected and reaches its target allocation.

Making timely and wise financial decisions requires keeping up with global events, economic trends, and market conditions. Reputable sources of financial news, research reports, and analysis can offer insightful information and assist you in keeping up with changes that could affect your portfolio. Furthermore, utilizing the knowledge and experience of financial advisors or investment specialists can provide individualized counsel and direction catered to your unique requirements and objectives.

When creating and maintaining an investing portfolio, taxes are a major factor. You may maximize your tax strategy by being aware of the tax ramifications of various investment accounts, including taxable brokerage accounts, individual retirement accounts (IRAs), and 401(k) plans. Choosing investments and tactics to reduce tax burden, such as holding tax-advantaged accounts, harvesting tax losses, and picking investments with advantageous tax treatment, is known as tax-efficient investing. Maximizing after-tax returns and navigating complicated tax laws can both be made easier by working with a tax professional.

Behavioral finance emphasizes the significance of controlling emotions and biases in investing, as it examines the psychological aspects impacting investment choices. Typical biases that might cause poor financial decisions include loss aversion, herd mentality, and overconfidence. These biases can be lessened by adopting a disciplined investing approach, concentrating on long-term objectives, and refraining from making snap judgments based on transient market swings. Long-term success requires having a well-defined investing plan and adhering to it, especially during volatile market times.

To sum up, creating an investing portfolio is a complex process that calls for a thorough comprehension of investment concepts, well defined goals, and rigorous assessment of risk tolerance. In order to manage risk and maximize returns, diversification across a range of asset classes, industries, and geographical areas is necessary. Keeping up with market circumstances, managing your portfolio regularly, and taking tax consequences into account are all essential to staying in line with your financial objectives. You can build a solid investment portfolio that satisfies your long-term financial goals and offers financial stability by following a disciplined strategy and utilizing the knowledge of financial experts.

Opening a Brokerage Account

A vital first step for anyone wishing to interact with the financial markets and actively engage in investing is opening a brokerage account. Investors can purchase and sell a variety of financial instruments, including stocks, bonds, mutual funds, ETFs (Exchange-Traded Funds), and more, using a brokerage account. Brokerage firms support this account. Depending on the sort of brokerage selected, these firms serve as a middleman between investors and the larger financial markets, giving access to trading platforms, research tools, and investment advice.

The first step in opening a brokerage account is usually choosing a brokerage company that best suits the investor's requirements and tastes. Brokerages come in a variety of formats; full-service brokers give comprehensive advising services, while discount brokers offer less fees for self-directed trading platforms. A number of variables, including the investor's expertise level, desired level of support, trading frequency, and financial goals, frequently influence the decision.

In order to begin the process of creating an account, potential investors must fill out an application that the brokerage business of their choice provides. The name, address, date of birth, Social Security number (or comparable identification number), employment position, income level, and investment objectives of the investor are among the vital personal data that this application gathers. Investors might also need to be specific about the kind of account they want to open, such as a joint account, individual account, retirement account (like a Traditional IRA or Roth IRA), or school savings account (like a 529 plan).

Brokerage businesses usually carry out identity verification and compliance checks following the application submission to make sure all legal criteria are fulfilled and to prevent fraud. Submission of copies of identifying documents, such as a passport, driver's license, or other government-issued ID, together with proof of address, such as a utility bill or bank statement, may be required as part of this verification procedure.

Upon approval and verification of the account application, investors fund their brokerage account. While funding methods differ from brokerage firm to brokerage firm, options like wire transfers, bank transfers, electronic funds transfers (EFT), and check deposits are frequently used. Transfers of securities from another brokerage account may also be accepted as a means of funding by certain brokerage firms.

Investors are granted access to the trading platform or online portal of the brokerage firm upon successful funding. With the tools and resources available on these platforms, investors may conduct due diligence on potential investments, examine market patterns, track the success of their portfolios, and place real-time trades. Whether they want to day trade, make long-term investments, or construct a diversified portfolio, investors can purchase and sell assets based on their investment strategy and preferences.

Monitoring account activity, keeping an eye on investment holdings, analyzing trade confirmations and statements, and evaluating portfolio performance are all part of managing a brokerage account. Regular account statements from brokerage businesses include information on transactions, dividend income, interest received, and any fees paid. To monitor the success of their investments and make sure their financial objectives are being fulfilled, investors are urged to periodically evaluate these statements.

In conclusion, for investors hoping to take part in the financial markets and gradually accumulate money, creating a brokerage account is a crucial first step. Investors can successfully manage the complexity of investing and work towards reaching their financial goals by selecting a brokerage firm that meets their needs, completing the application procedure, financing the account, and making use of the tools and resources offered. A brokerage account gives people the access, flexibility, and chances they need to expand their investments and confidently manage their financial futures.

CHAPTER III

Fundamental Analysis

Understanding Financial Statements

Investors, analysts, and stakeholders must comprehend financial statements in order to evaluate a company's financial performance and overall health. Financial statements are thorough reports that offer information on an organization's financial position, operations, and activities during a given time period. The three primary financial statements are the balance sheet, income statement, and cash flow statement. Each has a specific function in assessing various facets of a business's financial performance.

The balance sheet, sometimes referred to as the statement of financial status, shows a company's financial situation as of a particular date. It gives a quick overview of the company's equity held by shareholders, liabilities, and assets. Everything that a business possesses or has control over and has economic value is considered an asset, including money, stock, real estate, machinery, and equipment. Liabilities are the commitments and debts the business owes to third parties, such as loans, accounts payable, and accumulated costs. The corporation's net worth is reflected in the equity held by shareholders, which is the remaining interest in the entity's assets after liabilities have been subtracted.

The income statement, sometimes known as the profit and loss or P&L statement, is a financial document that lists a company's receipts, outlays, profits, and losses for a given period, usually quarterly or yearly. It starts with the overall revenues of the business, which come from the sale of products or services. It subtracts several costs, including taxes, interest, operational expenses, and cost of goods sold (COGS). The outcome is the net income or net loss, which shows whether the business made or lost money during the period.

The cash flow statement gives an overview of the inflow and outflow of cash and cash equivalents for a specific time period. It divides cash flows into three primary categories: financing, investment, and operational operations. Cash flows from the central business operations, such as supplier payments and customer receipts, are operating activities. Cash flows from investments in securities and the acquisition or disposal of long-term assets like property, plant, and equipment are examples of investing activities. Financial flows from debt repayment, dividend payments to shareholders, and capital raising are all included in financing operations.

A company's financial performance and health can be partially understood by examining its financial statements using critical financial ratios and measures. Quick and current ratios are examples of liquidity ratios that evaluate a company's capacity to pay short-term debt with its current assets. The ability of the business to turn a profit from sales and operating expenses is measured by profitability ratios like net profit margin, operating profit margin, and gross profit margin. Debt ratios that assess a company's leverage and ability to pay off debt include the debt-to-equity ratio and the interest coverage ratio.

Moreover, to ensure the accuracy and trustworthiness of financial data, financial statements are prepared in strict compliance with generally accepted accounting principles (GAAP) or International Financial Reporting Standards (IFRS). These standards, which are designed to guarantee uniformity and comparability in financial reporting, set rules and guidelines for how financial information is recorded, summarized, and presented in financial statements. This adherence to accounting principles should reassure stakeholders and investors that they can make educated decisions based on reliable financial data.

Your role in interpreting financial statements is crucial. A thorough understanding of the underlying business activities, industry dynamics, economic conditions, and accounting rules is necessary for this task. By using ratio analysis, trend analysis, and comparative analysis, you can assess a company's performance in relation to that of its competitors and industry norms. Evaluating the quality of earnings, cash flow creation, and overall financial health allows you to appraise the company's growth possibilities, profitability potential, and financial risks. Your expertise in these areas is what enables you to make informed decisions and contribute to the company's long-term financial success.

In summary, the power to evaluate a company's financial performance, position, and stability lies in your hands, as it requires a comprehension of financial statements. By carefully examining the balance sheet, income statement, and cash flow statement, you can gain a deep understanding of the company's assets, liabilities, revenues, expenses, and cash flows. Metrics and financial ratios further empower you to assess operational effectiveness, liquidity, solvency, and profitability. Ultimately, this competent financial statement interpretation enables you to see opportunities, reduce risks, and make well-informed decisions that will lead to long-term financial success.

Analyzing Company Performance

Evaluating a company's operations, financial standing, and competitive landscape are just a few of the many facets of the complex process that goes into analyzing its performance. Managers, investors, and other stakeholders must be aware of a company's performance to make wise judgments. This essay will explore the various approaches utilized to evaluate a company's success, such as ratio analysis, trend analysis, financial statement analysis, industry comparison, and qualitative aspects.

Analyzing financial statements is essential to comprehending the performance of a company. The cash flow statement, income statement, and balance sheet are a company's three primary financial statements that offer comprehensive information about its operations and economic situation. A company's assets, liabilities, and shareholders' equity are displayed on its balance sheet, which provides a moment-in-time view of the company's financial situation. The income statement, which includes information on revenues, expenses, and net income, shows the business's profitability over time. The cash flow statement shows the company's liquidity and cash management by tracking the inflows and outflows of cash. When taken as a whole, these claims aid analysts in evaluating the company's profitability, operational effectiveness, and financial stability.

By computing important financial ratios, ratio analysis is a potent tool for interpreting financial statements. These ratios offer a rapid means of assessing several facets of an organization's operations. The quick and current ratios are examples of liquidity measures that assess a company's capacity to pay short-term debt. The current ratio, which shows if the company has adequate assets to pay off its short-term debts, is computed by dividing current assets by current liabilities. By removing inventories from current assets, the fast ratio offers a stricter gauge of liquidity. The ability of the business to produce a profit in relation to its sales, assets, or equity is evaluated by profitability ratios such as the gross margin, operating margin, and return on equity (ROE). The efficiency of production and pricing strategies is indicated by the gross margin, which is computed by dividing gross profit by revenues. Operational efficiency is represented by the operating margin, which is calculated by dividing operating income by revenues. The ratio of return on equity (ROE), which is computed by dividing net income by shareholders' equity, indicates how well a company uses its equity to produce profits.

Financial leverage and the company's capacity to pay off debt are assessed using leverage ratios, such as the debt-to-equity and interest coverage ratios. The percentage of debt utilized to finance the company's assets is shown by the debt-to-equity ratio, which is computed by dividing total liabilities by shareholders' equity. A more excellent ratio indicates a riskier financial situation. The interest coverage ratio evaluates the ability of the business to pay interest by dividing operational income by interest expense. A more excellent ratio indicates more extraordinary ability to service debt. Efficiency ratios evaluate how well the business manages its assets. Examples of these ratios are the accounts receivable and inventory turnover ratios. The cost of goods sold (COGS) divided by the average inventory yields the inventory turnover ratio, which shows how quickly inventory is depleted and replenished. An increased ratio denotes effective inventory control. The speed at which the business receives money from clients is indicated by the accounts receivable turnover ratio, calculated by dividing net credit sales by average accounts receivable. A more excellent ratio indicates more efficient credit and collection procedures.

Trend analysis compares a company's financial performance across time to spot patterns and trends. This analysis aids in determining if the company's performance and economic status are improving, getting worse, or staying the same over time. For instance, a trend toward sales and net income growth over a number of years indicates that the business is expanding and turning a profit. On the other hand, a declining tendency can point to possible problems that require attention. Setting reasonable financial goals and predicting future performance are two different uses for trend analysis.

Benchmarking, also known as industry comparison, compares a company's performance to that of its rivals or peers. Understanding the company's competitive position in the industry and determining its relative strengths and weaknesses are made easier with the aid of this comparison. Benchmarking frequently makes use of key performance indicators (KPIs) like profit margins, market share, and revenue growth rate. Stakeholders can determine if the business is succeeding or underperforming in comparison to its rivals by examining these KPIs. A company may have a competitive edge in cost control or price strategy, for instance, if its profit margins are better than those of its competitors in the industry. Lower margins, on the other hand, can be a sign of inefficiencies or increased expenses.

Analyzing the performance of a corporation also heavily relies on qualitative elements. These elements include market conditions, competitive advantages, brand reputation, and management caliber. The caliber of its management can strongly impact the performance of a firm. Proficient leaders can stimulate creativity, execute tactical plans, and adeptly handle difficulties. A manager's leadership style, track record, and strategic vision are all taken into consideration while evaluating them. An additional important qualitative component is brand reputation. A powerful brand can increase client loyalty, demand higher prices, and differentiate the business from rivals.

Moreover, competitive advantages like strong patents, exclusive technology, or a vast distribution network might help achieve better results. The competitive landscape, governmental regulations, economic trends, and other market factors all affect how successfully a company performs. A comprehensive understanding of these qualitative aspects offers insight into the potential and hazards facing the company.

The SWOT analysis (Strengths, Weaknesses, Opportunities, Threats) is valuable for assessing qualitative issues. While opportunities and threats are external, strengths and weaknesses are internal considerations. A robust consumer base, an effective supply chain, or a strong brand are strengths. A narrow choice of products, a high debt load, or dependence on a small number of essential clients could be areas for improvement. Possibilities include creating new products, breaking into untapped markets, or taking advantage of advantageous regulatory adjustments. Economic downturns, heightened competition, and technological changes are examples of potential threats. One way to determine strategic priorities and opportunities for improvement is to conduct a SWOT analysis.

Knowing macroeconomic data is crucial in addition to the approaches mentioned above to analyze corporate performance. Macroeconomic variables affecting a company's performance include GDP growth, interest rates, inflation, and unemployment. These variables also have an impact on the larger business environment. For instance, businesses may see an increase in demand for their goods and services during times of economic expansion, which would result in more sales and profits. On the other hand, businesses may experience lower consumer spending, more stringent lending requirements, and higher cost pressures during economic downturns. Making wise strategic decisions and comprehending the external elements influencing the company's success are facilitated by keeping an eye on these indicators.

When assessing a company's success, investor mood and market circumstances are also critical factors to consider. In addition to a company's fundamentals, investor expectations and market mood affect stock prices. Market trends, trading volumes, and stock price fluctuations can all be used to analyze and gain insights into how the market views a company. Stock prices can rise in response to bullish market conditions and positive emotions but fall in response to bearish market conditions and negative sentiment. When one is aware of the market sentiment, it is easier to evaluate the opportunities and risks of investing in the company.

Innovation and technological developments are becoming increasingly significant considerations when evaluating a company's performance. Businesses that support new technologies and engage in research and development (R&D) frequently have a competitive advantage. Innovation can spur development and profitability by creating new goods, better workflows, and better consumer experiences. Analyzing a company's R&D spend, patent portfolio, and strategic objectives is part of evaluating its innovation commitment. Regularly innovating businesses can better adjust to shifting market conditions and hold onto their competitive edge.

Ethical standards and corporate governance are essential for assessing a company's performance. Robust internal controls, a transparent reporting system, and a well-organized board of directors are solid corporate governance procedures that improve decision-making and accountability. Sustaining the environment, treating workers fairly, and using ethical sourcing are all factors in building a company's long-term profitability and reputation. Examining a company's governance framework, rules, and performance history is necessary to evaluate its governance and ethical practices. Businesses prioritizing good governance and moral behavior are likelier to win over stakeholders' trust and protect their brand.

To sum up, measuring a company's performance is extensive and includes evaluating qualitative aspects, comparing industry benchmarks, studying financial statements, doing ratio analyses, and trend analyses. Analysis of financial statements sheds light on a business's cash flow, profitability, and overall health. Ratio analysis computes critical financial ratios to aid in interpreting these statements. Understanding competitive position, predicting future performance, and spotting trends are all made more accessible with trend analysis and industry comparison. A comprehensive understanding of the company's potential and hazards is provided by qualitative elements such as market circumstances, competitive advantages, brand reputation, and quality of management. Making informed decisions also requires knowledge of investor mood, technology developments, company governance procedures, and macroeconomic factors. By using these techniques, stakeholders can make strategic decisions that promote long-term success and obtain a thorough understanding of a company's performance.

Valuing a Stock

Finding the intrinsic worth of a company's shares is the first step in the fundamental stock valuation process, which is part of investing. This valuation is essential for making well-informed investing decisions because it enables investors to determine whether a stock is reasonably priced in the market, undervalued, or overvalued. Stock values can be determined using a variety of techniques and models, each with its own set of guiding ideas and practical uses. The most popular methods include dividend discount models (DDM), relative valuation, discounted cash flow (DCF) analysis, and fundamental analysis.

Stock valuation is based on fundamental analysis. A review of its financial statements, industry standing, competitive environment, and general economic conditions is necessary to determine a company's intrinsic value. This approach considers several variables: earnings, revenue, growth potential, and managerial caliber. Analysts usually begin by reviewing their income statement, balance sheet, and cash flow statement to learn more about a company's financial performance and position. Important indicators of a company's profitability and effectiveness include return on equity (ROE), price-to-earnings (P/E) ratio, and earnings per share (EPS).

The discounted cash flow (DCF) analysis is one of the most thorough techniques used in fundamental analysis. DCF entails projecting future cash flows for the business and applying a discount rate to reduce those flows to their present value. The weighted average cost of capital

(WACC) of the company, which considers the price of debt and equity financing, is frequently represented by the discount rate. The fundamental idea behind DCF is that a stock's value equals the total of its future cash flows, discounted to account for its current value. This approach necessitates a deep comprehension of the business model, sources of income, costs, and possibilities for expansion of the organization. Although DCF is widely recognized for its accuracy, it can be complicated and susceptible to many assumptions on future development and discount rates.

Comparable company analysis, often known as relative value, is another popular strategy. Using this approach, the valuation parameters of the target company are compared to those of comparable businesses operating in the same sector. The price-to-book (P/B) ratio, enterprise value-to-EBITDA (EV/EBITDA) ratio, and P/E ratio are frequently used measures. By analyzing these ratios, investors can ascertain whether the target stock is undervalued or overvalued by its rivals. For example, a firm may be undervalued and represent a possible purchase opportunity if its P/E ratio is lower than the average for the industry. On the other hand, variations in the growth rates, profitability, and risk profiles of the enterprises under comparison must also be considered when determining comparable worth.

Using the dividend discount model (DDM) to value stocks that pay dividends is incredibly beneficial. The foundation of this approach is the idea that a stock's value is equal to the present value of all of its potential dividend payments. The Gordon Growth Model, the most basic type of DDM, assumes that dividends will increase continuously. The formula used by the model to determine the stock's worth is $P = D / (r - g)$, where P stands for the stock price, D for the projected dividend per share, r for the needed rate of return, and g for the dividend growth rate. DDM is simple to use and implement, but it functions best for businesses with consistent dividend payments and steady growth rates.

In stock valuation, earnings per share (EPS) is crucial. The company's net income is divided by the number of outstanding shares to arrive at EPS. It shows the profit margin on each share of stock and is frequently used to assess the profitability of a business. A company with a greater EPS is usually more profitable, which might result in a higher stock price. The P/E ratio, which contrasts a company's current share price with its per-share earnings, also depends heavily on EPS. The P/E ratio helps determine if a stock is overvalued or undervalued by revealing how much investors are prepared to pay for a dollar of earnings.

The price-to-book (P/B) ratio, which contrasts a company's market value with its book value, is another crucial metric. The balance sheet is the source of the book value, which indicates the company's net asset value. The stock's market price is divided by its book value per share to get the P/B ratio. Given that the stock's market price is less than the company's net assets, a P/B ratio of less than 1.0 may suggest that the stock is cheap. On the other hand, a high P/B ratio can indicate that the stock is too expensive. The P/B ratio does not consider intangible assets or potential future growth; hence, it should be used with other indicators.

Another helpful statistic for assessing equities is the enterprise value-to-EBITDA (EV/EBITDA) ratio, especially in sectors where businesses have different capital structures. The market capitalization plus debt, minority interest, and preferred shares fewer total cash and cash equivalents is the calculation of enterprise value (EV). Earnings before interest, taxes, depreciation, and amortization, or EBITDA, is a metric used to assess how well a business is running. The valuation of a company, including debt, is compared to its actual cash earnings using the EV/EBITDA ratio. This ratio is frequently used in mergers and acquisitions analysis and is especially helpful for comparing businesses with varying debt levels.

Apart from these quantitative techniques, qualitative aspects are also fundamental in stock valuation. The business's competitive edge, management group, market trends, and macroeconomic circumstances are some of these variables. Substantial competitive advantages, such as distinctive products, devoted customer bases, or cutting-edge technology, can help a business continue to develop and be more profitable. Assessing the caliber and background of the management team can also reveal information about how well the business can carry out its plan and overcome obstacles. The performance and growth prospects of the company may be impacted by industry trends, including shifts in consumer preferences, technology advancements, and regulatory changes. Interest rates, inflation, and economic growth are macroeconomic factors affecting stock prices and the overall market environment.

Comprehending investor behavior and market sentiment is also crucial for determining stock value. The general perception that investors have of a particular stock or the stock market at large is known as market sentiment. Stock prices can rise in response to positive emotion and fall in response to negative sentiment. Numerous elements, including news, earnings reports, economic data, and geopolitical events, impact investor behavior. The study of behavioral finance examines how biases and psychological variables influence investing decisions. Overconfidence, herd mentality, and loss aversion are examples of common biases. Investors can avoid typical errors and make more logical decisions about their investments by being aware of these biases.

Determining a stock's value is a complex but necessary step in making wise investment choices. Understanding a

levels of considerable selling pressure. Technical analysts predict that as the price approaches a resistance level, selling pressure will likely increase, and the price may reverse downward.

Technical analysis relies heavily on chart patterns because they offer visual representations of investor mood and market psychology. A typical chart pattern is called "head and shoulders," and it has three peaks: the main peak, called the head, is higher than the two peaks that surround it, called the shoulders. This pattern is seen as a reversal pattern, suggesting that the trend may shift from being bullish to being bearish or the other way around. An additional pattern that is commonly acknowledged is the "double top" and "double bottom." When the price dips twice before turning back down, forming a double top, it indicates a bearish reversal. On the other hand, a bullish reversal is indicated by a double bottom, which occurs when the price strikes a support level twice before turning back upward.

Indicators and oscillators are additional tools used by technical analysts to enhance price charts and pinpoint possible entry and exit locations. These indicators are mathematical computations that indicate overbought or oversold situations, trend strength, momentum, and possible trend reversals. They are based on historical price and volume data. The moving average is a widely utilized indicator that reveals the underlying trend by smoothing out price data. When a short-term moving average crosses above or below a long-term moving average, it's known as a "moving average crossover," and it's sometimes taken as an indication that the trend is changing.

The Moving Average Convergence Divergence (MACD), which detects shifts in momentum based on the connection between short-term and long-term moving averages, and the Relative Strength Index (RSI), which gauges the pace and change of price moves, are two other well-liked indicators. To determine if a situation is overbought or oversold, oscillators like the Commodity Channel Index (CCI) and the stochastic oscillator are employed. When deciding whether to purchase or sell a security, technical analysts can use these indicators to validate patterns shown in price charts.

Another crucial element of technical analysis is volume analysis. The quantity of shares or contracts traded over a given time frame is known as the trading volume, and it offers information about how strongly or weakly prices are moving. Significant price fluctuations are frequently accompanied by high trading volume, which suggests substantial investor interest and validates price patterns. On the other hand, a low trading volume could indicate that traders are not as confident in the sustainability of price fluctuations and that they lack confidence.

To improve their analysis, technical analysts look at more than just specific signs and patterns; they also look at larger market trends and moods. Trend analysis, for instance, entails determining if price fluctuations are primarily moving in one of three directions: upward, downward, or sideways (consolidating). Technical analysts can tailor their trading techniques to suit the prevailing trend by having a clear understanding of the short-term (days to weeks), intermediate-term (weeks to months), and long-term (months to years) trends.

The general attitude of investors toward a specific market or securities is referred to as market sentiment. Sentiment indicators quantify investor sentiment and market volatility. Examples of these indicators are the put/call ratio and the VIX (Volatility Index). Because more investors are buying put options—which bet on price declines—than call options— which bet on price increases—a high put/call ratio indicates a pessimistic mood among investors. On the other hand, a low put/call ratio denotes optimism. The VIX, sometimes referred to as the "fear gauge," gauges investor uncertainty and market volatility. When the VIX is high, the market is usually more volatile and fearful, and when it is low, investors are likely calm and complacent.

There are drawbacks and restrictions to technical analysis. Technical analysis has its detractors who claim that it depends too much on past price data and trends, which makes it difficult to forecast future price movements, particularly in the event of unforeseen market events or shifts in the state of the economy. Additionally, various technical analysts may come to different conclusions due to the subjective nature of reading charts and indicators.

For traders and investors looking to comprehend market dynamics and make timely decisions based on price trends, patterns, and indicators, technical analysis is still a useful tool, even in the face of these criticisms. Through the integration of technical and fundamental analysis, together with a deep comprehension of market psychology, investors can enhance their comprehension of the market and increase the likelihood of accomplishing their investing goals.

Key Technical Indicators

Traders and analysts rely heavily on technical indicators to understand market dynamics and make wise judgments in the financial markets. These indicators provide insights into market trends, momentum, volatility, and possible reversals. They are mathematical computations from past price, volume, or open interest data. The Moving Average (MA) is an often-used fundamental indicator. By removing short-term volatility, MAs smooth out price data over a predetermined time period, assisting traders in identifying trends. The exponential moving average (EMA) and the simple moving average (SMA) are two popular MAs. In order to indicate shifts in the direction of the trend, traders frequently search for crosses between various moving averages (MAs), such as the 50-day and 200-day MAs. For example, when a shorter-term moving average crosses over a longer-term MA, it indicates growing momentum and possible upward price movement. This is a bullish indication.

In technical analysis, oscillators are just as important as trend-following indicators like MAs. Relative Strength Index (RSI) and other oscillators analyze the rate and direction of price changes to determine if an investment is overbought or oversold. The average gains and losses over a given time period—typically 14 days—are used to compute the relative strength index or RSI. Overbought situations are usually indicated by RSI values above 70, which may indicate a possible price reversal or retreat. On the other hand, oversold circumstances are indicated by RSI levels below 30, which suggests that prices may shortly return. Traders use the RSI to validate trends and predict future market-turning moments.

The Moving Average Convergence Divergence (MACD), which comprises the MACD and signal lines, is another well-liked oscillator. The longer-term EMA is subtracted from the shorter-term EMA to get the MACD line. The MACD line's EMA serves as the signal line. Crossovers between the signal line and the MACD line can indicate changes in the trend direction. A bullish momentum is indicated when the MACD line crosses above the signal line, and a bearish momentum is shown when it crosses below the signal line. Furthermore, the intensity of the trend can be inferred from the distance (also known as the MACD histogram) between the signal line and the MACD line.

By examining trade volume dynamics, volume indicators—like On-Balance Volume (OBV)—complement price-based indicators. Depending on whether the price closes higher or lower than the previous day, OBV increases or decreases the volume of a security. Growing OBV suggests significant purchasing pressure and may support a price increase. On the other hand, a decreasing OBV indicates selling pressure and a potential downward trend. Volume indicators aid traders in determining whether price movements are legitimate and spot probable trend continuations or reversals.

Bollinger Bands are an important tool for traders that concentrate on volatility. Bollinger Bands comprise an upper and lower band based on standard deviations of price movements and a simple moving average, usually with 20 periods. In response to changes in market volatility, the upper and lower bands grow and shrink, getting wider during high volatility and narrower during low volatility. When prices cross outside the bands, traders use Bollinger Bands to spot breakout chances or reversal signals when prices move back toward the moving average.

Another technical tool for determining possible support and resistance levels based on the Fibonacci sequence is the Fibonacci retracement levels. The basis for these levels is the ratios (23.6%, 38.2%, 50%, 61.8%, and 100%) that indicate important levels where price corrections or reversals may occur. Fibonacci retracement levels are a tool traders use to validate possible entry and exit positions in the market, along with other technical indicators.

Technological developments in the last few years have broadened the application of technical analysis beyond conventional indications. Artificial intelligence and machine learning algorithms are increasingly used to evaluate enormous volumes of market data and spot intricate patterns that human analysts would miss. By improving technical analysis's precision and speed, these cutting-edge technologies give traders access to actionable data and predictive models that help them manage risk and improve their trading tactics.

Technical analysis methods have evolved, but their effective use still necessitates a sophisticated grasp of investor psychology, market dynamics, and economic factors affecting price movements. Traders frequently combine technical indicators with fundamental and market sentiment analyses to obtain a complete picture of the market environment. By combining these methodologies, traders can make better decisions about position sizing, market entry and exit points, and overall portfolio management.

To sum up, technical indicators are essential tools that analysts and traders use to navigate the intricacies of the financial markets. These indicators enable traders to make well-informed decisions based on data-driven analysis by offering insightful information about market trends, momentum, volatility, and possible reversals. Technical analysis will become more popular as technology develops, providing traders with more advanced tools to improve their decision-making and adjust to shifting market conditions.

Developing a Trading Strategy

The process of creating a trading strategy, while laborious, is also empowering. It involves careful planning, analysis, and adjustment to market conditions. A trading strategy is a methodical way to purchase and sell financial instruments with the goal of making money while minimizing risk. Any good trading strategy starts with clearly identifying its objectives and aims. Traders need to ascertain their time horizon for transactions, expected return on investment, and risk tolerance.

Throughout the trading process, these characteristics aid in forming the overall strategy and direct decision-making, giving traders a sense of control and capability.

In-depth investigation and analysis are essential to creating a trading plan. To assess possible market opportunities, traders usually apply both technical and fundamental analytical methods. Fundamental analysis evaluates economic data, corporate financials, market movements, and geopolitical events to determine a security's intrinsic value. Based on the underlying qualities of the asset, it assists traders in determining whether it is overvalued or undervalued.

Technical analysis, on the other hand, examines past price and volume data to predict future price changes. Technical analysts utilize a range of instruments and indicators, including Bollinger Bands, relative strength index (RSI), and moving averages, to discern market trends, momentum, and possible turning points. Combining these assessments gives traders a thorough grasp of market dynamics and the ability to decide when to enter and leave transactions.

An essential part of any trading strategy is risk control. Traders use a variety of risk management strategies to safeguard funds and reduce losses. This involves reducing possible losses by putting stop-loss orders in place to exit trades if prices go against their expectations automatically. Another important component of risk management is position sizing, where traders use their risk tolerance and the likelihood of success to calculate how much capital to put into each trade. Traders can further reduce the risks associated with specific securities or sectors by diversifying across several asset classes and markets.

Developing a trading strategy also involves a lot of psychology. Mental toughness and emotional self-control are necessary qualities for profitable trading. Fear and greed are two examples of strong emotions that might impair judgment and cause impulsive judgments, which could compromise trading results. Traders frequently create psychological techniques, such keeping a trading record to analyze previous transactions and spot trends in their decision-making. Additionally, in order to lessen the impact of emotions during times of market turbulence or unforeseen events, they follow predetermined trading rules and techniques.

Another crucial aspect of successful trading techniques is adaptability. Technological developments, geopolitical events, and economic considerations all have an impact on markets, which are dynamic and always changing. Traders need to be adaptable and prepared to change course when the market conditions do. This could entail updating risk management procedures, improving technical indicators, or looking for new trading opportunities in developing industries or asset classes. By remaining knowledgeable and adaptable, traders can profit from market movements and maintain a competitive edge in the financial markets, instilling a sense of preparedness and confidence.

A trading strategy must be refined and validated through back testing and forward testing. Using previous market data, back testing allows you to evaluate the strategy's success under different market scenarios. This aids traders in assessing the strategy's long-term stability, profitability, and drawbacks. Forward testing, also known as paper trading, is the practice of making simulated trades in real time without risking real money. It enables traders to test the strategy's viability in the present market conditions prior to investing real money.

Optimizing and fine-tuning a trading strategy is a continuous process that requires ongoing observation and assessment. Traders frequently examine performance indicators including win-loss ratios, average profit per trade, and maximum drawdowns to pinpoint their advantages and disadvantages. To obtain insights into market patterns and enhance decision-making processes, they might use analytical tools and software, engage in trading groups, ask mentors or peers for comments, or use other strategies. This commitment to continuous improvement can motivate traders and keep them on the path to success.

Last but not least, sustained patience and discipline are essential for long-term trading success. Only some trades will be profitable, and markets can be unexpected. Traders need to stay true to their pre-established plans, avoid chasing trends or going against their risk-management guidelines, and have reasonable expectations for returns. Over time, traders can accomplish their trading objectives and traverse the complexity of financial markets by developing a disciplined approach and consistently improving their knowledge and skills.

To sum up, creating a trading strategy is a detailed and iterative process that includes establishing precise goals, carrying out in-depth investigation and analysis, successfully managing risks, upholding psychological discipline, and adjusting to shifting market conditions. In the cutthroat world of financial markets, traders can increase their chances of success and establish a long-lasting trading career by combining technical and fundamental analysis, putting robust risk management procedures into place, and regularly assessing and improving their tactics.

CHAPTER V

Investment Strategies

Long-Term Investing

Long-term investing is not just a strategic approach to wealth accumulation and financial security, it's a powerful tool that empowers individual investors. It prioritizes sustained growth over extended periods, allowing investors to take control of their financial future. Long-term investing is the process of purchasing and holding assets for years or even decades, as opposed to short-term trading, which focuses on profiting from sudden price swings. Using the potential of compound returns over time, the main goals of long-term investment are to achieve considerable capital appreciation and to create income in the form of dividends or interest payments.

Patience is one of the core values of long-term investing. Investors choose a buy-and-hold approach because they think that, in spite of volatility and short-term swings, markets appreciate over time. Investors can weather market downturns and profit from the historical pattern of markets rising over protracted periods of time by keeping a long-term outlook. This technique emphasizes stability and regularity in portfolio growth, in contrast to the high-frequency trading and speculation common in shorter-term strategies.

By distributing risk throughout several asset classes, industries, and geographical areas, diversification is essential to long-term investing. Investors can lessen the effect of specific market swings on their overall investments by diversifying their portfolios. Depending on their time horizon, investment objectives, and risk tolerance, they distribute funds among a variety of stocks, bonds, properties, and alternative assets. In addition to reducing volatility, diversification increases the chance of reaching long-term financial objectives and successfully manages risk.

Reputable fundamental analysis and study are necessary to find suitable long-term investment prospects. Before making an investment, investors consider an asset or company's competitive position, growth potential, financial stability, and management skill. To ascertain an investment's intrinsic worth, fundamental research includes reviewing financial accounts, estimating earnings potential, examining market patterns, and assessing macroeconomic factors. This thorough study allows investors to find inexpensive assets that meet their long-term investing goals and have significant growth potential.

Another important factor in long-term investing is income generating. Consistent dividend or interest payment streams that allow investors to benefit from both possible capital appreciation and a steady income stream are frequently given priority by investors; for long-term investors seeking growth and income stability, dividend-paying equities, bonds, real estate investment trusts (REITs), and premium corporate bonds are attractive options. Compounded growth over time can be further enhanced by reinvesting dividends and interest profits through dividend reinvestment plans (DRIPs) or automated reinvestment.

An essential component of long-term investing methods is risk management. Although there are inherent risks associated with all investments, wise investors use a variety of risk mitigation strategies to protect their money and reduce the likelihood of losses. A balanced risk-return profile that aligns with investors' financial objectives and risk tolerance is maintained with asset allocation, diversification, and regular portfolio rebalancing. In addition, having a long-term view, creating an emergency fund, and setting specific investment goals all help to reduce emotional reactions to market volatility and promote disciplined decision-making over time.

Environmental, social, and governance (ESG) factors are included in long-term investing. When choosing assets, responsible investing techniques prioritize ethical norms, sustainability, and corporate governance principles. ESG criteria assess how a business affects the environment, local communities, worker welfare, and shareholder rights. Long-term investors can support businesses dedicated to sustainable practices and reduce risks related to environmental, social, and governance challenges by incorporating ESG criteria into their investment decisions.

Long-term investing has become more than just a strategy, it's a community. Thanks to technological developments and information availability, regular investors are no longer on the sidelines, but are active participants in the investment world. They have access to tools and resources that were previously only available to institutional investors, allowing them to make well-informed decisions and effectively manage their assets. Real-time market data, research reports, and portfolio management tools offered by online brokerage platforms, robo-advisors, and investing apps are at their fingertips. These digital solutions not only offer various investment options catered to customers' preferences and financial goals, but also streamline the investment process and lower costs, making the audience feel included and part of the investment community.

Achieving personal financial goals and ensuring future financial security are two additional goals of long-term investing in addition to financial gains. Long-term investors place a high value on consistency, discipline, and resilience —whether they are saving for retirement, paying for school, or creating wealth for future generations. By adhering to a well-defined investment plan, upholding a diverse portfolio, doing comprehensive research, and remaining steadfast in their pursuit of long-term objectives, investors can effectively seize growth opportunities and navigate market setbacks, providing a sense of security and confidence in their financial future.

A long-term investment is a wise strategy for gradually accumulating money and reaching financial independence. Long-term investors can successfully traverse the intricacies of financial markets and take advantage of possibilities for wealth creation and preservation by focusing on sustained growth, diversification, income production, risk management, and good investing practices. Investors can increase their chances of success and guarantee a prosperous financial future for themselves and future generations by exercising patience and discipline and developing a clear investment strategy that aligns with their financial objectives.

Short-Term Trading

A dynamic and active way to trade on the financial markets, short-term trading focuses on taking advantage of quick price changes and market inefficiencies over brief time frames. Short-term trading seeks to profit from volatility and momentum in various asset classes, such as stocks, currencies, commodities, and derivatives, in contrast to long-term investing, which emphasizes gradual wealth generation over years or decades. Individuals and institutional traders who want to make quick profits by creating and selling purchases and sales quickly—often in a matter of hours, days, or even minutes—find this trading technique appealing.

Technical analysis, which forecasts future price movements by analyzing past price data and market statistics, is one of the main techniques used in short-term trading. To spot patterns and trends in asset prices, technical traders employ a range of instruments and indicators, including Bollinger Bands, relative strength index (RSI), and moving averages. With the use of these indicators, traders can decide whether to enter or leave positions based on overbought/oversold circumstances, trend reversals, and momentum indications. Short-term traders use technical analysis to try and forecast short-term market changes and profit chances.

The most well-known type of short-term trading is day trading, defined as placing several trades in a single trading day and closing all of your positions before the market shuts. Day traders seek to profit from intraday price movements caused by market news, economic releases, or technical patterns. They concentrate on liquid assets with high trading volumes. Quick decision-making, in-the-moment market analysis, and disciplined risk management are necessary for this technique to capitalize on short-term opportunities while minimizing potential losses effectively.

Another standard short-term trading method is swing trading, which keeps positions open for a few days to a few weeks to profit on price swings or momentum trends that occur within longer market cycles. Swing traders seek to profit from expected price moves during brief market volatility by analyzing technical charts and indicators to pinpoint possible entry and exit opportunities. Swing trading, as opposed to day trading, enables traders to manage risk by setting profit objectives and stop-loss orders while capturing bigger price swings and trends over somewhat longer time frames.

Scalping is a very active and quick short-term trading method in which traders make many trades throughout the day in an attempt to profit from little price swings. In order to make additional profits, scalpers concentrate on liquid assets with narrow bid-ask spreads. They enter and exit positions in a matter of seconds to minutes. This approach uses sophisticated order execution tools, high-frequency trading methods, and real-time market data access to take advantage of the market's transient price disparities and inefficiencies.

Risk management is a critical aspect of short-term trading due to its inherent volatility and quick market fluctuations. Traders follow strict risk management procedures, setting stop-loss orders to minimize potential losses and adhering to position sizing guidelines to control the amount of capital allocated to each trade. Diversifying trading tactics among different asset classes or marketplaces can further disperse risk and maximize returns under various market conditions.

Short-term traders frequently employ margin trading and leverage to increase possible returns. With leverage, traders can borrow money from a broker to take control of larger positions with a smaller amount of cash. Leverage can improve earnings, but if trades move against expectations, it also raises the danger of suffering big losses. Similarly, margin trading is borrowing money from a brokerage to trade assets; traders must maintain a minimum margin requirement and may be subject to margin calls if positions experience substantial losses.

Short-term trading requires emotional regulation and psychological self-discipline for success. The fast-paced environment of short-term trading can trigger emotions such as fear, greed, and anxiety, which can cloud judgment and lead to impulsive actions. To maintain focus and control in volatile market conditions, traders often adopt psychological measures such as keeping a trading journal, following set trading guidelines, and engaging in mindfulness exercises.

Short-term trading has become more accessible to the general public thanks to technological developments and the growth of Internet trading platforms. Individual investors now have access to sophisticated trading tools, algorithmic trading tactics, and real-time market data that were previously only available to institutional traders. In order to take advantage of short-term opportunities and maximize trading success, short-term traders can now execute transactions quickly, evaluate market patterns with accuracy, and automate trading techniques.

Finally, short-term trading, which focuses on taking advantage of sudden price changes and market inefficiencies across a range of asset classes, is a dynamic and active way to trade in the financial markets. Short-term traders seek to make quick profits while navigating the inherent volatility and complexity of short-term market dynamics by utilizing technical analysis, disciplined risk management, and modern trading tools. Even while this trading technique has the potential to yield large profits quickly, long-term success, in the long run, will need a strategic approach, psychological fortitude, and constant adjustment to shifting market conditions.

Alternative Strategies

Investing alternatives comprise a broad spectrum of methods that depart from conventional long-only stock and fixed-income investments. These approaches are intended to provide special chances for yielding returns, controlling risk, and expanding portfolio diversification beyond traditional asset classes. In order to improve portfolio performance and reduce market volatility, institutional investors, hedge funds, and sophisticated individual investors are drawn to alternative methods, which sometimes entail non-traditional asset classes, derivatives, or intricate investment structures.

Hedge funds are a well-known example of alternative methods. They use a variety of investing strategies to generate positive returns independent of market conditions. In order to profit on market inefficiencies and price disparities, hedge funds frequently take both long and short positions in stocks, bonds, currencies, and commodities. In addition to using leverage, arbitrage, and derivatives trading, these funds may also use risk management approaches such as hedging to increase profits. Hedge funds serve institutional and accredited investors, providing opportunities for portfolio diversification and higher returns than traditional investing.

Another important alternative method is private equity, which focuses on investing in privately held businesses or buying shares in publicly traded corporations to grow, reorganize, or revive operations to create value. Private equity companies raise money from high-net-worth individuals and institutional investors to finance acquisitions and strategic initiatives. Compared to public equities, these investments frequently have more extended holding periods, enabling businesses to carry out growth initiatives, operational enhancements, and strategy realignment to optimize returns over time. Investors in private equity may benefit from significant cash gains and access to opportunities not found in open markets.

Venture capital is a specific type of private equity investment intended to support startups and growth-stage businesses with significant room for expansion, especially in the biotechnology, technology, and other creative industries. In return for stock ownership, venture capitalists give startup companies funding, mentoring, and strategic advice. Because these investments are made in early-stage enterprises, there is a greater chance of failure, but if the companies are successful, there might be large profits. By financing innovative concepts and game-changing technologies with the potential to transform markets and ultimately generate enormous amounts of value, venture capital is critical in promoting entrepreneurship and innovation.

Investing in physical properties, real estate securities, and assets related to real estate can yield income and capital appreciation. A wide variety of alternative ways are included in real estate investment strategies. Without direct ownership of real estate assets, real estate investment trusts (REITs) give investors access to diversified portfolios of income-generating assets like office buildings, retail establishments, residential complexes, and industrial facilities. Real estate investment trusts (REITs) provide investors with attractive returns and substantial tax advantages by distributing a sizable amount of their income to them as dividends.

Alternative investment techniques centered on trading physical commodities or financial derivatives contracts connected to commodity prices are represented by commodities and managed futures. Natural resources like gold, crude oil, agricultural products, and industrial metals are examples of commodities. Systematic trading based on quantitative models and algorithms intended to identify patterns in equities indexes, commodity prices, interest rates, and currency values is the foundation of managed futures strategies. These strategies appeal to institutional investors and portfolio managers looking to control risk and improve portfolio efficiency because they offer benefits linked to diversification, protection against inflation, and possible returns that are not correlated with traditional asset classes.

Through liquid and transparent vehicles, alternative mutual funds and exchange-traded funds (ETFs) provide individual investors with access to alternative investment methods. These funds can potentially invest in alternative asset classes such as commodities, real estate, private equity, and hedge fund-like techniques. Retail investors have the opportunity to diversify their portfolios, protect themselves from market downturns, and improve risk-adjusted returns by using alternative mutual funds and exchange-traded funds (ETFs). By providing daily liquidity and regulatory monitoring, these vehicles help individual investors who want to diversify and manage risk in their investing portfolios by making alternative methods more accessible and manageable.

Given that alternative investing strategies can be more sophisticated, leveraged, and volatile than standard investment methods, the role of risk management becomes crucial. Institutional investors and fund managers employ advanced risk management techniques, quantitative analysis, and scenario planning to evaluate and reduce risks associated with alternative strategies. Diversification, asset allocation, hedging, and dynamic portfolio rebalancing are some of the strategies that assist in controlling downside risk and maximizing portfolio performance in a variety of market conditions.

As investors increasingly incorporate sustainability criteria into their decision-making processes, the importance of environmental, social, and governance (ESG) factors in the context of alternative investment strategies is growing. Responsible investing strategies, when selecting alternative investments, prioritize social impact, environmental stewardship, and corporate governance requirements. ESG integration is a powerful tool that promotes sustainable growth, ethical business conduct, and long-term value generation for stakeholders and investors. It achieves this by aligning financial objectives with larger societal goals, a key aspect of alternative investment strategies.

To sum up, alternative investing strategies comprise a wide range of methods intended to improve portfolio diversity, control risk, and generate profitable returns outside of traditional asset classes. These techniques, which range from venture capital and hedge funds to real estate, commodities, and commodities, give institutional investors and well-educated people access to niche markets, let them benefit from specialist knowledge, and help them negotiate changing market conditions. Alternative investments contribute significantly to portfolio creation by offering possible sources of alpha, income generation, and inflation protection within a diversified investment framework despite their inherent risks and complexity.

Alternative strategies will likely remain essential to the investment landscape, providing creative answers to meet changing investor needs and preferences, as long as investors seek ways to maximize risk-adjusted returns and match their investments with larger societal and environmental objectives.

CHAPTER VI

Behavioral Finance

Understanding Investor Psychology

Grasping the behaviors, emotions, and cognitive biases that influence investment decisions and market dynamics is a challenge and an opportunity for empowerment. Understanding investor psychology, the psychological elements that shape people's perceptions, actions, and beliefs in the financial markets, can significantly enhance risk tolerance, decision-making procedures, and overall investing results.

The idea of risk aversion and tolerance is one of the cornerstones of investor psychology. An investor's willingness and capacity to withstand changes in the value of their investments is referred to as their risk tolerance. Individual differences exist because of time horizon, income stability, financial goals, and prior market volatility experiences. Contrarily, risk aversion refers to an investor's propensity to favor safer, less volatile investments over riskier ones, even when the latter have larger potential rewards. Building a balanced investment portfolio that fits one's comfort level and long-term goals requires understanding one's risk tolerance.

The behavioral finance theory sheds light on how emotions and cognitive biases affect investing choices. Investors may make irrational decisions based more on feelings than objective analysis due to behavioral flaws such as confirmation bias, loss aversion, and herd mentality. For example, loss aversion describes an investor's propensity to dread losses more than they value gains, which can result in cautious investing choices or panic selling during market downturns. Confirmation bias is the tendency for investors to ignore contradicting data in favor of information that supports their preexisting ideas, which can result in skewed investing decisions.

Investor psychology is heavily influenced by emotions, which affect traders' decisions to purchase and sell in the financial markets. Fear and greed are two common emotions that influence investor behavior and market cycles. Greed drives investors to seek out more significant profits and take on greater risk during bull markets, which are marked by rising prices and optimism. In contrast, fear rules during bear markets, which are characterized by declining prices and pessimism, driving investors to sell their assets and run for cover quickly. Asset prices and the stability of the market as a whole can be impacted by emotional reactions to market swings that magnify volatility and cause illogical market movements.

Another psychological characteristic that may influence investing choices is overconfidence. Overconfident investors frequently overestimate their expertise, know-how, and capacity for precise market forecasting. They might ignore diversification rules, trade excessively, or take on unnecessary risks because they think they can outperform the market on a regular basis. If overconfidence is not restrained by humility, objective analysis, and a realistic appraisal of one's abilities and limitations, it can result in lousy investment outcomes.

Investor and market sentiment are essential components of investor psychology that impact price movements and market trends. Market sentiment, which is frequently influenced by economic statistics, geopolitical developments, corporate earnings reports, and central bank policies, is the general attitude of investors toward a given market or asset class. While negative sentiment can result in selling pressure and price drops, a positive mood in the market can stimulate buying activity and drive asset values higher. Contrarily, investor sentiment influences both market behavior and investment decisions by reflecting individual investors' attitudes, feelings, and expectations toward future market circumstances.

The tendency of investors to follow the herd rather than make their own decisions based on primary research is known as herd mentality. When investors rush to acquire or sell assets based on the behaviors of others rather than a logical appraisal of asset values, herding behavior frequently causes market bubbles and crashes. Herd mentality can lead to inefficiencies and increased market volatility since prices may differ from intrinsic values because of group behavior rather than underlying causes.

Financial counselors and investment professionals play a pivotal role in managing the psychology and behavior of investors. They are not just advisors, but guides who navigate clients through emotional market cycles, help them make informed investing decisions, and most importantly, provide the reassurance and support needed to stay disciplined. By offering information, direction, and customized plans based on each person's risk tolerance, financial objectives, and time horizons, they assist clients in reducing the effects of behavioral biases and achieving long-term investing outcomes.

Through real-time access to trading platforms, research tools, and market information, technology, and digital platforms have completely changed the mindset of investors. For individual investors, robo-advisors, smartphone trading apps, and online brokerage accounts provide ease, transparency, and customized investing options. These technical developments increase transparency and lessen emotional biases in investing decisions by enabling investors to make data-driven judgments, execute transactions effectively, and track the success of their portfolios in real-time.

To sum up, navigating the complexity of financial markets and attaining excellent investing outcomes requires understanding investor psychology. Investors who understand how emotions, cognitive biases, and market sentiment impact their decisions are better able to implement disciplined strategies, efficiently manage risk, and keep a long-term perspective. Optimizing investment returns and eliminating behavioral biases require financial education, objective analysis, and cooperation with trusted advisors in a dynamic and constantly shifting global marketplace.

Strategies to Mitigate Biases

Strategies to mitigate biases are crucial in decision-making processes across various domains, including finance, medicine, psychology, and everyday life. Cognitive biases are systematic patterns of departure from reason or objective judgment. They frequently persuade people to base their decisions not on logic or factual information but on subjective considerations. These prejudices have the potential to produce unfavorable results, poor decision-making, and judgment errors. Bias recognition and mitigation are critical to increase cognitive performance, promote justice, and improve decision accuracy.

A useful tactic to lessen prejudices is raising awareness and educating people. People might become more aware of their own mental processes and inclinations when they are educated about typical cognitive biases and their effects. Being conscious enables people to identify situations in which biases can affect their decisions and encourages them to use more logical, fact-based methods. Bias education can be incorporated into professional training programs, organizational development projects, and academic curricula to promote a culture of cognitive awareness and critical thinking.

Using frameworks for decision-making that promote systematic information processing and evaluation is another crucial tactic. Decision matrices, decision trees, and checklists are examples of structured decision-making frameworks that assist people in gathering information, weighing options objectively, and considering various viewpoints. These frameworks encourage rational thinking, evidence-based assessment, and uniform standards for evaluating options, reducing the impact of biases, and offering an organized decision-making method. People can lessen the impacts of confirmation bias, anchoring effects, and overconfidence bias by adhering to formal frameworks.

Thirdly, by embracing a range of experiences, opinions, and points of view, encouraging diversity and inclusiveness in decision-making helps reduce biases. Diversity promotes innovative problem-solving, challenges presumptions, and lessens groupthink, improving decision-making. People are more inclined to confront consensus-driven judgments and biases in diverse teams and organizations, producing more comprehensive and well-rounded results. Decision-makers can lessen biases associated with stereotyping, similarity bias, and group attribution mistakes by actively soliciting feedback from people with various backgrounds, cultures, and levels of competence.

Furthermore, promoting a psychologically safe atmosphere is essential to reducing biases in settings where decisions are made. A psychologically secure environment is one in which people feel free to express their thoughts, pose inquiries, and question accepted wisdom without worrying about criticism or retaliation. People are more inclined to express different viewpoints, engage in productive debate, and speak up about potential biases in psychologically safe circumstances. Leaders and managers must value constructive criticism, promote open communication, and respect opposing viewpoints to foster psychological safety.

Another practical method for reducing biases is to use data-driven decision-making techniques. Thanks to data analytics and quantitative approaches, decision-makers can now base their choices on empirical data, statistical analysis, and predictive modeling. By utilizing data-driven insights, people can reduce biases associated with availability heuristics, representativeness bias, and anecdotal reasoning. When decisions are based on scientific data rather than personal opinions or gut feelings, data-driven decision-making encourages objectivity, accuracy, and accountability.

Encouraging accountability and close examination of decisions, and decision-making procedures with solid peer review and feedback channels can also help reduce biases. Peer review invites peers or subject matter experts to assess choices made, question presumptions, and offer helpful criticism based on their knowledge and viewpoints. Peer review procedures bring extra scrutiny, a variety of perspectives, and a critical assessment of the reasoning behind decisions, which aid in identifying and correcting biases. Organizations can improve decision-making processes and lessen the influence of biases by implementing peer review.

In addition, bias mitigation in dynamic and changing situations requires cultivating a culture of ongoing learning and adaptation. A growth mindset should be adopted by decision-makers, who should strongly emphasize continuous learning, experimentation, and modification in response to feedback and fresh data. People who engage in constant learning can better stay current with information, refute outmoded assumptions, and modify their decision-making processes in response to shifting conditions. Organizations can attenuate prejudices associated with status quo bias, sunk cost fallacy, and resistance to change by encouraging a culture of learning and adaptation.

Fairness, transparency, and integrity in decision-making processes are three more ways ethical norms and decision-making principles can provide a foundation for reducing biases. Decision-makers can be guided by a set of rules and principles known as ethical guidelines, guaranteeing that decisions are made with stakeholders' best interests in mind. By upholding ethical standards, people can lessen biases associated with moral hazard, ethical fading, and self-interest bias. Frameworks for ethical decision-making promote responsibility, tolerance for difference, and analysis of broader societal effects.

In summary, methods to reduce biases are critical for raising the accuracy of decisions, encouraging justice, and boosting cognitive efficacy across a range of domains. People and organizations can lessen the impact of biases on decision-making processes through the following strategies: developing cognitive awareness; putting in place structured decision-making frameworks; encouraging diversity and inclusion; building psychologically safe environments; utilizing data-driven approaches; incorporating peer review mechanisms; embracing continuous learning; and abiding by ethical guidelines. These tactics not only reduce the dangers of biased decision-making but also promote an innovative, moral, and critical-thinking culture that helps achieve the best results in various situations.

The Role of News and Media
The media and news play a vast and complex role in the stock market, influencing market patterns, investor sentiment, and overall financial decision-making. The news media, which includes digital and social media platforms in addition to more conventional media like

radio, television, and newspapers, is a significant source of information and analysis that influences consumer behavior and perceptions on a daily basis.

First and foremost, news and media are essential for spreading knowledge about company earnings reports, economic data, and geopolitical events that affect financial markets. News sources are essential for investors to remain up to date on macroeconomic information, including central bank interest rate decisions, jobless claims, GDP growth, and inflation rates. These economic indicators impact investor mood and market direction by offering insights into the state of the economy and possible future trends.

Corporate news and earnings announcements significantly impact stock prices and market volatility. Companies frequently disclose financial results, quarterly earnings reports, and guidance updates through press releases and conversations with the media. Stock prices might climb in response to positive earnings surprises or robust revenue growth, piquing investor interest and fostering a bullish outlook on the market. On the other hand, poor financial results or unfavorable press—such as lawsuits, government inquiries, or management changes—may cause sell-offs and a drop in stock values.

How the media presents international news and geopolitical events influences investor confidence and market mood. Financial markets can become unstable due to political unrest, trade disputes, natural disasters, and foreign conflicts. As a result, investors may need to reevaluate their risk tolerance and modify their investment plans. The media provides real-time updates and analysis on these occurrences, which shapes public perceptions of market risk and affects asset values in different markets and geographical areas.

News media sites publish market commentary and analysis by economists, financial experts, and business professionals. These sources offer insights and viewpoints on possible hazards, investment possibilities, and market trends. Analysts provide forecasts, stock recommendations, and sector outlooks based on fundamental analysis, technical indicators, and market trends. When making investing decisions, investors frequently take these observations into account. They also seek advice on market timing tactics, portfolio diversification, and asset allocation.

Digital platforms, social media, and traditional media outlets have revolutionized the way financial news and information are disseminated. Investors can get real-time updates, market comments, and viewpoints from various sources through blogs, forums, social networking sites, and online financial news websites. Investors can respond quickly to breaking news and market events, exchange market insights, and discuss investment strategies on social media sites like LinkedIn, Twitter, and financial discussion groups.

The phenomena of "market news impact" has been attributed to the speed and accessibility of news dissemination through digital and social media platforms. Quickly spreading information can set off quick reactions in the financial markets, resulting in intraday swings and price volatility. In times of increased uncertainty, algorithmic trading systems, and high-frequency trading (HFT) algorithms are designed to respond in milliseconds to news headlines and market sentiment, magnifying market fluctuations and intensifying volatility.

For investors, hazards and difficulties are associated with the widespread dissemination of news and media. Investors may need help to separate factual news from conjecture and noise due to information overload caused by the constant stream of news and the proliferation of information sources. Investors who depend on reliable information to make decisions face dangers when misinformation, rumors, and fake news spread on social media platforms skew market views and cause illogical market reactions.

The emotions of investors and the market dynamics are also impacted by psychological variables and behavioral biases caused by media coverage. Herd mentality can accentuate market trends and lead to asset bubbles or market declines because it causes investors to follow the activities of others instead of doing their independent research. Sensationalized media coverage can cause fear of losing (FOL) and fear of missing out (FOMO), which can fuel excessive exuberance during bull markets or panic selling during market downturns, respectively, and influence short-term market volatility.

Market sell-offs and extended periods of volatility can be caused by negative emotions and weakened investor confidence created by media coverage of financial scandals, market crashes, and economic downturns. Critical thinking, due diligence, and maintaining a long-term investment perspective are crucial amid media-driven narratives and short-term market volatility. The financial media has a significant role in influencing public perception and mood.

Regulatory bodies and trade associations have a part to play in maintaining truth, openness, and investor protection in media coverage of the financial markets. The purpose of laws prohibiting insider trading, market manipulation, and the spread of inaccurate or misleading information is to protect investor confidence in financial markets and preserve market integrity. Before making investing decisions based on market speculation or media reports, investors are advised to use caution, double-check information, and confer with financial advisors.

In summary, news and media play a critical role in the stock market by affecting market patterns, investor attitudes, and financial decision-making. News sources offer up-to-date information, intelligent analysis, and knowledgeable commentary on business and economic news, geopolitical developments, and market patterns that affect asset values and volatility. Investors must overcome the obstacles of information overload, media bias, and psychological biases to make logical, disciplined investment decisions that align with their financial objectives and risk tolerance, even while media coverage improves transparency and makes informed decision-making easier.

CHAPTER VII

Risk Management

Identifying Different Types of Risk

To make wise financial decisions and implement efficient risk management techniques in a variety of investment vehicles and financial markets, it is essential to recognize the different forms of risk. When discussing investments, the risk is the uncertainty or likelihood of loss or other unfavorable events that could have an impact on the value or projected returns of an asset. Investors may evaluate possible risks, put appropriate risk mitigation strategies in place, and make well-informed decisions that align with their financial goals and risk tolerance by thoroughly understanding the many types of risk.

Market risk, usually called systemic risk, is one of the main categories of risk that investors encounter. All investments within a particular asset class or market segment are subject to market risk, including the potential for losses due to more general economic reasons and market volatility. Financial indicators (including GDP growth, inflation rates, and interest rates), geopolitical developments, and worldwide market patterns affect market risk. All investments are subject to some market risk, which can only partially be eliminated by diversification or individual asset selection.

Interest rate risk is another important kind of risk that is especially pertinent to fixed-income investments like bonds. Interest rate risk is the possibility that shifts in interest rates will have an effect on bond yields and prices. Bond prices usually decrease when interest rates rise and vice versa. Consequently, after acquiring fixed-rate bonds, bondholders risk decreasing market value if interest rates rise. Investors can reduce interest rate risk by selecting floating-rate bonds, diversifying bond maturities, or matching bond durations to their investment time horizons.

Credit risk, also known as default risk, is the chance that borrowers—governments, businesses, or private citizens—may be unable to fulfill their financial commitments, leaving lenders or bondholders with a loss. The credit risk is contingent upon the issuer's creditworthiness and the credit ratings bestowed by rating organizations, such as Standard & Poor's and Moody's. Investments with a greater risk profile, such as high-yield bonds or unrated debt securities, usually have a more significant potential return but a higher credit risk. By spreading their investments among several issuers, doing in-depth credit research, and keeping an eye on financial health metrics and credit ratings, investors can reduce their exposure to credit risk.

Liquidity risk is the inability to buy or sell an investment swiftly at a reasonable price because of a lack of market activity or trading volume. When liquidity circumstances worsen, illiquid investments—like some stocks, bonds, or alternative assets—may see significant bid-ask spreads and price volatility. When there is a market downturn or economic crisis, market players may be reluctant to trade, which could cause price dislocations and delayed asset sales. In these situations, liquidity risk is more important. Investors can reduce liquidity risk by diversifying their holdings among liquid and illiquid assets, keeping sufficient cash reserves, and routinely evaluating market liquidity circumstances.

Exchange rate variations that impact the value of investments denominated in foreign currencies give rise to currency risk, sometimes referred to as exchange rate risk. Currency risk arises when foreign investors or businesses operating internationally convert profits, dividends, or principal repayments to their home currency. Depending on whether the currency appreciates or depreciates about the investor's base currency, exchange rate fluctuations can have a favorable or negative effect on investment returns. Investors with foreign holdings can reduce their exposure to currency risk by using hedging tools like currency forwards or options.

Uncertainties resulting from alterations in governmental policies, laws, or geopolitical events that could impact investment values or operational activities are included in political and regulatory risk. Changes in trade tariffs, government stability, taxation policies, and geopolitical tensions that affect investor confidence and corporate operations are examples of political risk factors. The possible effects of new laws, rules, or compliance requirements on specific organizations, industries, or investments are referred to as regulatory risk. Investors can manage political and regulatory risk by completing political risk assessments, keeping up with legislative developments, and diversifying across jurisdictions or industries less vulnerable to regulatory changes.

Sustainability risk, also known as environmental, social, and governance (ESG) risk, takes into account how environmental, social, and governance concerns may affect investment performance and corporate sustainability. ESG risks include things like labor standards, corporate governance procedures, diversity and inclusion policies, resource scarcity, and climate change. ESG factors are becoming more and more important to investors as they evaluate a company's or investment portfolio's long-term sustainability, reputation risk, and regulatory compliance. ESG integration entails matching investment choices with responsible investing tenets, interacting with businesses on ESG practices, and integrating ESG criteria into investment analysis.

The possibility of a broad disruption or instability in the financial system that impacts several institutions or markets is called systemic risk. The interdependence of financial institutions, the ripple effects of a market crisis, or structural weaknesses in the financial system can all lead to systemic hazards. Situations like the 2008 global financial crisis brought to light the systemic dangers related to intricate financial instruments, high levels of leverage, and insufficient risk control procedures. To improve financial stability, lessen the impact of spillovers, and preserve the financial system's resilience, regulators and central banks keep an eye on systemic risk factors and put measures into place.

Operational risk is the possibility of suffering financial losses or disturbances as a result of insufficient internal procedures, mistakes made by employees, malfunctions with technology, or outside circumstances that affect how a business operates. All firms are vulnerable to operational hazards, including supply chain interruptions, fraud, cybersecurity attacks, and natural disasters. Investors assess the resilience plans and operational risk management techniques businesses have implemented to reduce operational risks and safeguard shareholder value. Resilient internal controls, backup plans, and disaster recovery plans are necessary for efficient operational risk management.

To sum up, investors must recognize the various forms of risk to comprehend and handle the intricacies of the financial markets and make wise investment choices. Investing in risk carries different risks and opportunities for those looking to maximize risk-adjusted returns, protect capital, and reach long-term financial objectives. In a dynamic and changing global economy, investors can manage uncertainties, seize opportunities, and create resilient portfolios suited to their risk tolerance and investment goals by identifying and evaluating potential risks, putting diversified investment strategies into practice, and using risk management techniques.

Techniques for Managing Risk

A crucial component of decision-making and operations in all fields, including business and finance, healthcare, engineering, and daily living, is risk management. Risk is the probability of unfavorable results or losses as a result of unknowns and unforeseen circumstances. Effective risk management includes recognizing, evaluating, prioritizing, and reducing risks to limit risks and maximize possibilities for attaining goals. In order to ensure resilience, continuity, and sustainable progress in both persons and organizations, a variety of tactics and strategies are used to manage risk proactively and methodically.

Identifying and evaluating risks is one of the main methods for risk management. This entails methodically locating possible hazards that have an impact on goals, initiatives, or operations. In addition to external causes like the state of the economy, alterations in regulations, and natural disasters, internal elements that can cause risks include organizational procedures, human error, or resource limitations. Risk assessment entails determining how likely each risk will materialize and any potential effects it might have on goals or results. To fully evaluate risks and rank them according to likelihood and severity, a combination of qualitative and quantitative approaches is employed, including risk workshops and expert judgment. Quantitative methods include probability analysis and sensitivity analysis.

Another risk management tactic is risk avoidance, especially in situations where a risk's possible costs or repercussions outweigh its advantages. Changing strategies, procedures, or actions to get around or completely remove a risk is known as risk avoidance. To prevent possible financial losses or operational interruptions, a business can decide not to pursue a high-risk initiative or enter a volatile market. Avoiding risk might be beneficial in some situations, but it can also stifle chances for development and creativity. Organizations must thus strike a balance between strategic goals, risk tolerance, and risk avoidance.

Reducing the possibility or impact of hazards that have been discovered entails taking preventative action and implementing controls. Mitigation methods aim to decrease the frequency or severity of hazards that are not entirely avoidable. Implementing strong internal controls, adding redundancy to crucial systems, diversifying suppliers or markets, and improving safety procedures are common risk mitigation strategies. Businesses could spend money on disaster recovery plans to lessen the effects of operational disruptions or cybersecurity measures to reduce the chance of data breaches. By implementing mitigation measures, organizations can strengthen their resilience against unanticipated events and decrease their susceptibility to risks.

Another risk management strategy is risk transfer, which involves assigning the financial repercussions of a risk to a different party. A typical kind of risk transfer is insurance, in which businesses or individuals pay insurance firms premiums in return for protection against certain risks such as property damage, liability claims, and business interruption. Businesses can shield themselves from large financial losses brought on by unforeseen circumstances beyond their control by shifting risks to insurers. To properly manage overall risk exposure, risk transfer only partially eliminates risks; coverage limits, exclusions, and deductibles must be carefully considered.

Organizations that intentionally choose to accept specific risks without taking further steps to reduce or transfer them are said to be using the risk acceptance strategy. When risks are judged acceptable within predetermined risk tolerance thresholds or when the expense of mitigating a risk exceeds the potential consequence, risk acceptance is commonly used. For instance, companies may take on reasonable operational risks related to regular business operations or market volatility if they are within their means. Risk acceptance necessitates monitoring and regular re-evaluation to ensure risks stay within reasonable bounds and do not suddenly increase, even though it does not actively reduce risks.

Planning for possible future events and uncertainties through scenario and contingency planning is a proactive approach to risk management. To predict how risks might materialize and affect goals, scenario planners create alternative scenarios or future predictions based on various hypotheses and factors. Organizations can efficiently minimize risks by identifying trigger points, early warning indicators, and potential solutions by examining a variety of scenarios. On the other hand, contingency planning entails creating predetermined plans of action and tactics to be put into place in the event that particular hazards come to pass. Plans for contingencies lay out how to keep things running smoothly, reduce interruptions, and lessen the negative effects of unforeseen circumstances on stakeholders.

Organizations must integrate risk management into their strategic planning and decision-making processes in order to achieve resilience and sustainable growth in a changing and unpredictable environment. Enterprise risk management (ERM) and other integrated risk management frameworks offer organized methods for detecting, evaluating, and handling hazards at every level of a business. By incorporating risk concerns into day-to-day operations, project planning, and resource allocation,

Enterprise Risk Management (ERM) frameworks facilitate accountability, promote transparency in decision-making, and connect risk management efforts with strategic objectives.

Real-time insights, predictive modeling, and scenario analysis are ways that technological improvements and data analytics help improve risk management capabilities by foretelling dangers and guiding decision-making. Organizations may effectively monitor important risk indicators, automate risk assessments, and centralize risk data by utilizing risk management tools and platforms. Using technology, organizations can improve their capacity to recognize new risks, address vulnerabilities, and respond to threats proactively and on time.

Last but not least, successful risk management requires developing a culture of risk awareness, accountability, and continual improvement. Leadership commitment, employee participation, and frequent training programs foster a standard knowledge of risks. Proactive risk detection and reporting are also encouraged, and people at all organizational levels are given the ability to participate in risk management initiatives. By instituting a risk-aware culture, organizations can improve their resilience, adaptability, and capacity to seize opportunities while skillfully handling possible dangers and uncertainties.

In summary, a thorough and proactive strategy for detecting, evaluating, prioritizing, and mitigating risks is necessary for effective risk management to maximize opportunities and accomplish strategic goals. Organizations may effectively manage uncertainties, increase resilience, and reduce vulnerabilities by implementing scenario planning, contingency planning, risk avoidance, mitigation, transfer, and acceptance strategies. In an increasingly complex and linked global context, integrated risk management frameworks, technology improvements, and a supportive organizational culture further enhance risk management capabilities. These factors help to ensure sustainable growth, continuity, and success in risk management.

Monitoring and Adjusting Your Portfolio

Monitoring and adjusting your portfolio is a critical aspect of investment management, essential for aligning your financial goals with market conditions and changing circumstances. A diverse collection of investments from a range of asset classes, including equities, bonds, mutual funds, exchange-traded funds (ETFs), real estate, and alternative investments, that are matched to your time horizon, financial goals, and risk tolerance make up a portfolio. However, the cornerstone of effective portfolio management is strategic asset allocation, which involves distributing your investments among various asset classes according to their correlation and risk-return characteristics. This strategic approach is key to optimizing your portfolio for long-term financial success. Monitoring effectively entails assessing your portfolio's performance, risk exposure, and alignment with your investing objectives on a frequent basis. Adjusting entails making calculated changes to improve returns, control risks, and adjust to changing market conditions.

Setting up a strategic asset allocation plan and specific investing goals is the first step in keeping an eye on your portfolio. Your financial goals, including capital preservation, income production, wealth accumulation, and retirement planning, are defined by your investment objectives. The distribution of your investments among various asset classes according to their correlation and risk-return characteristics is known as asset allocation. For stability and income, a cautious investor could allocate a more significant percentage of their portfolio to fixed-income assets; conversely, a growth-oriented investor might allocate a more critical part to stocks in order to benefit from long-term capital gains. Assessing whether your current asset allocation is in line with your risk tolerance and investing goals is the first step in the monitoring process.

It's critical to regularly assess performance in order to track the advancement of your portfolio toward your investing objectives. Performance measures encompass evaluating the total returns of a portfolio, contrasting actual results with benchmarks (market indices, peer group averages, etc.), and comparing the performance of individual investments to projections. However, equally important is the role of risk assessment and management in portfolio monitoring. This involves analyzing variables including market risk, credit risk, liquidity risk, and concentration risk across your investments. By understanding and managing these risks, you can protect the stability of your portfolio and its long-term goals. Performance analysis evaluates your investment strategy's efficacy and provides information for future modifications by taking into account variables including total return, volatility, yield, expense ratios, and tax consequences.

In order to detect and reduce possible risks that could jeopardize the stability of the portfolio and its long-term goals, risk assessment and management are essential components of portfolio monitoring. Analyzing variables, including market, credit, liquidity, and concentration risk across your investments, is part of risk assessment. Value at Risk (VaR), stress testing, and scenario analysis are some of the tools that may be used to assess the resilience of your portfolio and estimate possible losses in the event of a volatile market. Managing risk might include using hedging techniques to guard against downside risks, spreading your holdings across several industries and geographical areas, and routinely rebalancing your portfolio to meet targeted asset allocation criteria.

Aftermarket gyrations or shifts in investment values, rebalancing is a tactical adjustment approach used to realign your portfolio to its intended asset allocation. Due to different returns over time, asset classes may diverge from their initial weights, which can cause imbalances in portfolios and possible overexposure to particular assets. In order to restore the intended asset mix, rebalancing entails selling overperforming assets and redistributing the proceeds to underperforming or underweighted assets. Investors can maintain portfolio diversification, limit risk exposure, and capture gains by rebalancing on a regular basis, all of which help to ensure alignment with long-term investing goals.

In order to adapt your portfolio to shifting possibilities and external conditions, you must keep an eye on market and economic developments. Economic indicators that vary across different sectors and countries influence asset prices and market dynamics. These indicators include GDP growth, inflation, interest, and employment data. Investors can predict changes in the market, changes in the sectors they invest in, and new investment opportunities by keeping an eye on macroeconomic trends. For instance, during economic expansion, investors may become more exposed to cyclical industries like consumer discretionary and technology. At the same time, defensive sectors like utilities and healthcare may fare better during economic contraction.

To manage your portfolio to reduce geopolitical risks and take advantage of sector-specific possibilities, it is essential to stay up to date on geopolitical developments, regulatory changes, and industry-specific news. Global markets and asset prices can be impacted by geopolitical events, such as trade disputes, political unrest, or geopolitical tensions, which may require adjusting portfolio posture. Portfolio strategies may need to be adjusted due to regulatory changes, such as monetary policy changes or tax reforms, which may impact investment returns and tax consequences. News particular to a given industry, including technological advances or changes to healthcare regulations, may present hazards or investment possibilities that call for adjusting a portfolio to take advantage of new trends or reduce industry-specific risks.

Tax considerations heavily influence portfolio adjustments, which drive investment decisions aimed at maximizing after-tax returns and minimizing tax liabilities. Capital gains and taxable income can be mitigated by tax-loss harvesting, in which investors sell underperforming assets to incur capital losses for tax purposes. Investors can reduce or postpone paying taxes on capital gains and investment income by utilizing tax-advantaged accounts, like 401(k) plans or IRAs. Long-term wealth accumulation techniques are supported, and overall after-tax returns are optimized when portfolio allocations are adjusted with tax consequences in mind.

Portfolio adjustments are also heavily influenced by behavioral factors, including investor sentiment, market psychology, and emotional biases. These factors can significantly impact investment decisions, often leading to impulsive reactions to market trends or irrational decision-making. Understanding and managing these behavioral biases is crucial to maintaining a disciplined investment approach and avoiding emotional reactions to short-term market volatility. By doing so, you can effectively monitor and adjust your portfolio, reducing the potential for these biases to negatively impact your investment decisions. Reducing behavioral biases and improving consistency in decision-making can be achieved through engaging in mindfulness practices, keeping a diverse portfolio, and getting unbiased financial counsel.

To sum up, keeping an eye on your portfolio and making necessary adjustments are continuous procedures that are necessary to accomplish long-term investing goals, control risks, and maximize returns in volatile and dynamic markets. Monitoring performance, risk exposure, alignment with investing objectives, and risk tolerance are all critical components of an efficient portfolio. Making strategic decisions based on geopolitical changes, market conditions, tax implications, behavioral issues, and economic trends is necessary when adjusting your portfolio. Through the implementation of a disciplined approach, ongoing education about market dynamics, and flexibility in response to evolving conditions, investors can strengthen the durability of their portfolios, seize opportunities, and skillfully manage risks to attain financial success in the long run.

CHAPTER VIII

Tax Considerations

Understanding Investment Taxes

Investors must comprehend investment taxes in order to maximize after-tax profits, manage their portfolios skilfully, and adhere to tax laws. Because they affect investment decisions and lower overall returns, taxes can significantly affect the results of investments. Different tax treatments apply to different forms of investment income and transactions based on an investor's tax bracket, asset class, and holding duration, among other considerations. People can minimize their tax payments and maximize tax efficiency by making educated decisions based on their awareness of the tax implications of their investments.

Capital gains, or the income from selling assets like stocks, bonds, mutual funds, and real estate, are one of the main sources of investment taxes. Capital gains are classified as either long-term or short-term based on how long the asset is held. Ordinary income tax rates apply to short-term capital gains, which are gains on assets held for a year or less. These rates can be substantially higher than those for long-term capital gains. Long-term investment is encouraged by preferential tax rates on capital gains, which are normally lower than ordinary income tax rates on assets held for more than a year.

Another popular type of taxable investment income is dividend income. Distributions of profits made to shareholders by mutual funds and corporations are known as dividends. Investors benefit tax-wise since qualified dividends are taxed at long-term capital gains rates. Dividends from non-qualified investments, such as certain overseas investments and real estate investment trusts (REITs), are subject to regular income tax rates. Investors can evaluate the after-tax impact of dividend-paying investments on their portfolios by thoroughly understanding dividend categorization and tax treatment.

Bonds, CDs, savings accounts, and other fixed-income assets all have interest that is subject to ordinary income tax rates. State and local governments that issue tax-exempt bonds provide an advantage to taxpayers by shielding their interest income from federal income taxes. For investors looking for tax-efficient income in higher tax rates, municipal bonds, in particular, may be appealing. Assessing the post-tax yield of taxable and tax-exempt bonds enables investors to make well-informed choices on their investment goals and tax status.

Tax-loss harvesting is the practice of using realized investment losses to lower taxable income and offset capital gains. Within the same tax year, investors may deduct capital gains from additional investments made by selling underperforming assets at a loss. Any excess capital losses over capital gains can be carried over to subsequent tax years, allowing for an annual net capital loss deduction of up to $3,000 against ordinary income. Over time, tax-loss harvesting can reduce tax obligations and increase the overall tax efficiency of a portfolio.

Retirement accounts provide tax-advantaged benefits to encourage retirement savings. Examples of these accounts are Traditional IRAs, Roth IRAs, and employer-sponsored 401(k) plans. Generally, contributions to 401(k) and Traditional IRA plans are tax deductible in the year they are made, lowering the contributor's taxable income. However, withdrawals from 401(k) and Traditional IRA plans are liable to regular income tax in retirement. Conversely, Roth IRAs allow tax-free growth and, if certain requirements are satisfied, tax-free withdrawals upon retirement but do not offer upfront tax deductions for contributions. Comprehending the tax consequences associated with retirement accounts facilitates individuals in making efficient retirement plans and optimizing their retirement savings approach.

Due to their intricate structures and investing tactics, alternative investments—like hedge funds, private equity, and some real estate—may have particular tax implications. Carry interest, or income from private equity and hedge fund investments, is taxed as capital gains at special rates for fund managers. Specific tax laws, such as those pertaining to like-kind exchanges and depreciation deductions, apply to real estate investments, which include rental income and capital gains from property sales. Investors should speak with tax professionals to fully comprehend the unique tax ramifications and reporting obligations related to alternative investments.

Tax-efficient investing strategies aim to reduce taxes while maintaining portfolio diversification and investment returns. After-tax returns can be optimized using techniques like asset positioning, which entails putting tax-efficient investments in taxable accounts and tax-inefficient investments in tax-advantaged accounts. Asset sales, withdrawals, and contributions can also be used to rebalance portfolios and manage tax implications. To optimize the creation of after-tax wealth and reach long-term financial objectives, tax-efficient investing takes into account variables like investment time horizon, tax bands, and projected changes in tax regulations.

Another facet of investment taxes is estate planning, which reduces estate taxes and effectively manages the transfer of wealth to heirs and beneficiaries. If an estate exceeds a specific threshold, estate taxes may be applicable, often called inheritance taxes. The rates of these taxes vary depending on the jurisdiction and the deceased person's relationship to the taxpayer. Estate planning techniques can lower estate tax obligations and guarantee the orderly transfer of assets in accordance with personal preferences and family needs. These techniques include giving assets during one's lifetime, creating trusts, and using estate tax exclusions and deductions.

For investors to correctly report investment income, capital gains, and deductions to tax authorities, tax reporting and compliance are crucial duties. Maintaining thorough documentation of all investment transactions—including purchase prices, proceeds from sales, dividends paid, and distributions of capital gains—simplifies tax filing and helps ensure that taxable gains and losses are calculated accurately. To maximize after-tax returns and achieve long-term financial success, tax-efficient investment decisions and strategies must be continuously monitored and adjusted in response to changes in tax legislation, financial objectives, and market conditions.

To sum up, investors must have a solid understanding of investment taxes to successfully manage the complexity of tax regulations, maximize after-tax returns, and accomplish their financial goals. People can minimize taxes, maximize tax benefits, and improve portfolio performance by making educated decisions about the tax implications of various investment income streams, transactions, retirement accounts, alternative investments, and tax-efficient strategies. Financial advisors and tax experts can offer individualized advice and methods catered to specific situations, guaranteeing adherence to tax laws and maximizing tax efficiency in wealth management and investment planning.

Tax-Efficient Investing Strategies

Tax-efficient investing strategies are essential for investors seeking to maximize after-tax returns, minimize tax liabilities, and optimize overall portfolio performance within the framework of existing tax laws and regulations. These tactics cover a range of methods and factors to lessen the effect of taxes on capital gains, investment income, and overall portfolio growth.

One fundamental strategy in tax-efficient investing is asset location. The process of strategically moving investments among taxable and tax-advantaged accounts according to their respective tax characteristics is known as asset localization. Generally, taxable brokerage accounts are used to hold tax-efficient investments, like equities with qualifying dividends and long-term capital gains potential. This placement allows Investors to take advantage of lower tax rates on qualifying dividends and long-term capital gains. On the other hand, assets like bonds or actively managed funds that yield interest income, short-term capital gains, or large taxable payouts are best placed in tax-advantaged accounts like Traditional IRAs or 401(k) plans. Investors can reduce annual tax liabilities and improve after-tax returns over time by strategically placing assets.

The harvesting of tax losses is another successful tax-efficient tactic. Using this strategy, investments are sold at a loss to offset realized capital gains and lower taxable income. Investors may be able to make a capital loss on the sale of a security if its value drops below their original acquisition price. The investor's overall tax burden can be decreased by using the realized loss to offset capital gains realized in other parts of the portfolio. Any excess losses over $3,000 in a given tax year can be applied to ordinary income if capital losses exceed capital profits; any remaining losses can be carried forward to subsequent tax years. Tax-loss harvesting, especially in times of market downturns or asset price volatility, enables investors to manage their tax obligations better, rebalance their portfolios, and increase their after-tax profits.

Tax-efficient investment also involves making use of tax-advantaged retirement funds, such as 401(k) plans, Roth IRAs, and Traditional IRAs. Traditional IRA and 401(k) plan contributions are frequently tax deductible in the year made, lowering the contributor's taxable income. These accounts provide for tax-deferred growth of investments, which means that investors' earnings are only subject to taxation once they are taken after retirement. Roth IRAs allow for tax-free investment growth and distributions for eligible withdrawals if specific requirements are fulfilled. Investors can enhance long-term wealth accumulation and retirement savings by utilizing tax-advantaged retirement plans, which allow them to delay or eliminate taxes on investment returns and maximize the compounding of investment gains over time.

Because long-term capital gains tax rates are lower than short-term capital gains rates, investing over the long term is naturally tax-efficient. Long-term capital gains tax treatment is available to investments kept for more than a year; rates vary from 0% to 20% depending on the investor's filing status and taxable income. Investors who prioritize long-term investment horizons may be able to lower their overall tax burden and take advantage of advantageous capital gains tax rates. Long-term investing methods minimize taxable transactions and portfolio turnover while enabling investors to take advantage of compounding returns and market growth. They are also in line with wealth accumulation aspirations.

Another tax-efficient tactic to lower short-term capital gains taxes from frequent investment buying and selling is portfolio turnover management. Ordinary income tax rates, which can be substantially higher than long-term capital gains rates, apply to short-term capital gains. Investing using a buy-and-hold strategy reduces taxable transactions, postpones realizing capital gains, and maximizes after-tax earnings. A long-term investing focus and limiting pointless trading are two aspects of strategic portfolio management that assist investors in protecting capital and lowering tax obligations related to temporary gains.

Tax-efficient investment vehicles, such as index and exchange-traded funds (ETFs), can also benefit investors. These funds often have lower portfolio turnover and produce less taxable dividends than actively managed funds. By tracking industry-specific or broad market indices, index funds and exchange-traded funds (ETFs) offer diversified exposure to a variety of assets with minimal capital gains distributions. Investors can reduce their taxable income, postpone realizing capital gains, and eventually maximize their after-tax returns by making investments in tax-efficient funds. Furthermore, investors who live in the state where the municipal bonds (munis) are issued may be eligible for tax-exempt interest income at the federal and occasionally state levels for purchasing munis issued by state and local governments. Municipal bonds offer ways to successfully manage overall tax responsibilities, diversify fixed-income portfolios, and produce tax-free income.

To avoid inheritance taxes and tax-efficiently transmit wealth to future generations, high-net-worth individuals must engage in estate planning and gifting techniques as essential components of tax-efficient investing. Investors can transfer assets while lowering estate tax liabilities and optimizing tax benefits for recipients by using estate planning strategies, including creating trusts, donating to charities, and taking advantage of annual gift tax exclusions. By implementing tax-efficient estate planning measures, investors can safeguard their wealth, minimize tax implications, and guarantee a smooth distribution of their assets per their desires.

Lastly, successful tax-efficient investing requires keeping current on changes in tax laws, rules, and policies. Updates to capital gains tax rates, investment expense deductions, retirement account contribution caps, and tax reform laws can all affect investment strategies and need modifying tax planning techniques. To maintain compliance with tax legislation, traverse changing tax landscapes, and optimize tax-efficient investment strategies, investors should seek advice from financial advisors, tax specialists, and legal experts.

In summary, tax-efficient investment techniques are crucial for investors to reach their long-term financial goals, maximize after-tax profits, and reduce tax obligations. Investors can maximize portfolio performance and preserve capital in a tax-efficient way by carefully allocating assets, using tax-loss harvesting, leveraging tax-advantaged retirement accounts, emphasizing long-term investing, controlling portfolio turnover, investing in tax-efficient vehicles, putting estate planning strategies into practice, and remaining up to date on tax laws. In order to minimize the impact of taxes on investment returns and financial goals, investors can navigate market uncertainty, take advantage of investment opportunities, and accumulate wealth by applying tax-efficient investment methods and effective tax planning.

Working with Tax Professionals

For individuals and corporations, working with tax specialists is crucial to navigating the complexities of tax legislation, maximizing tax planning techniques, and guaranteeing regulatory compliance. Professionals in the tax field, such as tax attorneys, registered agents, and certified public accountants (CPAs), bring specialized knowledge and skills to the table. They provide crucial assistance and support customized to each client's needs and circumstances.

Working with tax specialists has several benefits, chief among them being their ability to offer knowledgeable tax planning guidance. They keep up with regular updates and changes to tax laws that can affect financial decisions, so they thoroughly understand all federal, state, and local tax requirements. Tax experts create customized tax plans to reduce tax obligations while optimizing available deductions and credits by evaluating their customers' financial circumstances, revenue sources, investments, and business operations. In addition to assisting clients in maximizing their tax efficiency, this proactive strategy guarantees legal compliance, lowering the possibility of audits and penalties.

When it comes to helping people and businesses prepare and file their taxes correctly, tax specialists are invaluable during tax preparation season. They ensure that all required schedules and forms are accurately filled out and timely submitted to the appropriate tax authorities. This painstaking attention to detail reduces the likelihood of mistakes and inconsistencies leading to audits or processing delays. In order to accomplish accurate and compliant tax reporting, tax professionals also apply their skills to interpret complicated tax laws and regulations and apply them effectively to each client's particular financial circumstances.

In addition to preparing taxes, tax experts provide year-round strategic tax planning services. They provide customers with important financial advice, taking into account the tax ramifications of each choice, on matters including investments, retirement planning, estate planning, and company transactions. Tax specialists assist clients in making well-informed decisions that are consistent with their long-term financial objectives by predicting possible tax results and strategically structuring transactions. Through proactive tax preparation, customers can minimize taxes and maximize their financial strategy, improving their overall financial well-being in the process.

Apart from preparing and budgeting taxes, tax experts can offer crucial support in handling tax-related matters and settling conflicts with tax authorities. In situations like audits, appeals, and negotiations with the Internal Revenue Service (IRS) or state tax authorities, they represent their customers' interests as advocates. Tax experts are skilled in interpreting and applying tax rules, putting out strong client arguments, and promoting just outcomes. Their representation gives customers peace of mind in potentially stressful situations by guaranteeing that their rights are upheld and that they are treated relatively under the law.

Tax specialists provide firms with specific services that extend beyond individual tax preparation and planning. They help companies manage the many tax ramifications associated with sales taxes, payroll taxes, corporation taxes, and foreign tax issues. Experts in taxation provide guidance on capital investments, business formation, M&A, and adherence to sector-specific tax laws. Tax experts aid in the optimization of tax strategies that promote expansion, profitability, and regulatory compliance by having a thorough awareness of the particular difficulties and opportunities that firms confront.

Another crucial area in which tax experts are essential is estate planning. They offer advice on how to set up estate plans to reduce estate taxes and guarantee that assets are systematically transferred to beneficiaries and heirs. Tax specialists assist people in utilizing tax-efficient techniques, including charitable giving and trusts, navigating complex estate and gift tax regulations, and maximizing available exemptions and deductions. Tax professionals assist clients in preserving wealth, safeguarding family legacies, and achieving their long-term financial goals by incorporating tax considerations into estate planning.

Beyond their technical knowledge, tax professionals are also responsible for upholding ethical standards, advocating for their clients, and engaging in continuous professional development. Professional associations like the National Association of Enrolled Agents (NAEA) and the American Institute of Certified Public Accountants (AICPA) have set strict ethical norms and standards of practice that they must abide by. In their dealings with clients, tax professionals respect the values of honesty, discretion, and responsibility, which builds client trust and confidence in their advising services.

To stay up to date with the latest tax laws, regulations, and industry trends, tax professionals must engage in continuous professional education. They take part in continuing education courses, workshops, and certifications to broaden their knowledge and expertise, which helps them to provide clients creative solutions and well-informed advice. Tax professionals adjust their practices to produce value-added services that satisfy the changing demands of individuals and businesses in a dynamic economic climate by staying ahead of legislative changes and technological improvements.

Working with tax professionals gives people and companies peace of mind because they know that their tax issues are handled skillfully and in accordance with the law. Clients benefit from tax professionals' specialized knowledge, attentive care, and proactive approach, whether they are seeking advice on ordinary tax problems, strategic financial planning, or complex tax issues. Through the application of their expertise, experience, and commitment to client achievement, tax professionals enable people and companies to meet financial objectives, overcome obstacles, and establish a strong base for sustained success.

In summary, hiring tax experts is a wise investment in both personal and corporate financial stability and compliance. Tax professionals assist customers maximize tax efficiency, reduce risks, and meet their long-term financial goals by providing significant experience in tax planning, preparation, compliance, and dispute resolution. Clients who work with tax specialists have access to proactive tactics, moral support, and individualized advice that improves financial decision-making and guarantees compliance with tax laws and regulations.

CHAPTER IX

Resources and Tools for Investors

Educational Resources

The complex and dynamic stock market requires a thorough understanding of effective participation and successful investment. The need for comprehensive educational materials has increased as more people and companies interact with the stock market. The knowledge and abilities needed to negotiate the complexities of stock trading and investing are provided by these resources, including books, online courses, seminars, financial news sources, and simulation programs. Access to high-quality educational resources enables investors to control risks, make wise decisions, and reach their financial objectives.

Books, which provide in-depth analysis, historical perspectives, and strategic insights into the stock market, have long been a mainstay of financial education. Value investing, market theories, and the concepts of risk and return are all covered in detail in classic texts like Burton Malkiel's "A Random Walk Down Wall Street" and Benjamin Graham's "The Intelligent Investor." The significance of careful investigation, prudent investing, and long-term viewpoints is emphasized in these texts. Modern works about investing that discuss current market dynamics, the emergence of index funds, and the effects of high-frequency trading include "The Little Book of Common-Sense Investing" by John C. Bogle and "Flash Boys" by Michael Lewis. Books provide insightful information on a variety of subjects, covering anything from behavioral finance and market psychology to technical and fundamental analysis, making them useful for both new and seasoned investors.

People can now learn about the stock market at their own pace and convenience thanks to online courses and educational platforms that have democratized access to this knowledge. There are a ton of courses available on websites like Coursera, Udemy, and Khan Academy about financial analysis, trading tactics, and stock market investing. These courses, which are frequently created by academic institutions and business professionals, cover a wide range of subjects, from advanced methods like options trading and quantitative analysis to the fundamentals of stock markets and investing strategies. Interactive elements like discussion boards, quizzes, and assignments improve the educational process by letting students apply ideas and interact with one another. Additionally, a lot of online platforms offer certification programs that attest to the knowledge and abilities learned, enhancing professional growth and career advancement.

Professionals from the industry, academics, and investors come together for interactive and immersive learning experiences at seminars, webinars, and workshops. These gatherings, which are frequently sponsored by investment businesses, financial institutions, and educational institutions, give attendees the chance to network with industry professionals, obtain useful insights, and keep current on trends and advancements in the sector. Attendees who attend seminars on subjects like portfolio management, risk assessment, and market forecasting leave with practical advice and tools to improve their investing methods. With the ease of learning from home and participating in live lectures, Q&A sessions, and real-time conversations, webinars may be accessible remotely. Through supervised exercises and case studies, participants at workshops—usually more hands-on—can delve extensively into certain areas of interest, such as technical analysis or retirement planning.

Media sites and financial news sources are essential for getting current and pertinent information on the stock market. Television networks such as CNBC, Fox Business, and Bloomberg provide in-depth coverage of financial news and events, professional analysis, and real-time market updates. Many publications, including financial times, Barron's, and the Wall Street Journal, provide in-depth coverage of investment opportunities, economic indicators, and market trends. Stock quotations, financial statements, analyst reports, and market commentary are just a few of the many tools available on online financial portals such as Yahoo Finance, MarketWatch, and Seeking Alpha. Investors can recognize developing possibilities and hazards, make smarter decisions, and respond quickly to market movements by staying informed through dependable news sources.

Using simulation tools and virtual trading platforms, investors can hone their trading skills in a risk-free environment. Users are able to replicate actual market conditions and make trades without taking on any financial risk thanks to platforms such as Investopedia's Stock Simulator, TD Ameritrade's paperMoney, and MarketWatch's Virtual Stock Exchange. Beginners can test investment strategies, become familiar with market mechanics, and learn from mistakes without losing money by using these tools, which are very helpful. Simulation tools assist investors in becoming more competent and confident by simulating real-world circumstances, so getting them ready for actual market involvement.

Online forums and investment clubs provide cooperative learning opportunities that encourage a sense of unity and information sharing among participants. Investment clubs offer an organized method of learning about the stock market. Typically, they are made up of a limited number of people who pool their resources and skills. Members get together on a regular basis to talk about market trends, exchange research, and decide on investments as a group. Online forums and communities like Seeking Alpha, Reddit, and StockTwits allow for peer-to-peer learning, discussion, and idea sharing. These forums give investors a place to talk about their experiences, get different viewpoints, and ask questions to understand the market better.

Governmental organizations and regulatory bodies also support investor education with a range of programs and materials. On its Investor.gov website, the U.S. Securities and Exchange Commission (SEC) provides a plethora of information on subjects like regulatory updates, fraud prevention, and investment fundamentals. The Financial Industry Regulatory Authority (FINRA) offers tools, resources, and instructional materials to assist investors in protecting themselves from fraud and making well-informed decisions. Through seminars, books, and online tools, government-sponsored initiatives like the SEC's Investor Education and Advocacy program seek to advance financial literacy and investor safety. Through these activities; investors are supported in their efforts to make wise financial decisions by having access to accurate, impartial, and trustworthy information.

Academic establishments and business schools, which provide degree programs, courses, and research possibilities in finance, economics, and investment management, are major players in the education of the stock market. Academic institutions like Stanford, Wharton, and Harvard offer extensive programs that address the quantitative techniques, theoretical underpinnings, and real-world applications of finance and investing. Through student-run investment funds, internships, and finance groups, students can participate in experiential learning and obtain practical expertise as well as industry insights. Scholarly investigations and written works enhance comprehension in domains including asset pricing, behavioral finance, and market efficiency, offering significant perspectives to decision-makers and practitioners alike.

Professionals in the sector might receive specialized education through corporate training programs and professional development courses provided by financial institutions and investment firms. These courses provide advanced instruction in subjects including asset allocation, risk management, and financial modeling and are intended for financial advisors, portfolio managers, and investment analysts. Professional legitimacy and career prospects are enhanced by rigorous training and accreditation offered by certification programs, such as the Certified Financial Planner (CFP) certification and the Chartered Financial Analyst (CFA) title. Financial professionals may maintain their competitiveness, relevance, and effectiveness by investing in ongoing education and professional development.

Digital technologies and technological developments have revolutionized stock market education, increasing its accessibility, interactivity, and interest. Mobile apps, podcasts, and video tutorials make learning about the stock market on the road easier. Apps with user-friendly interfaces for trading, investing, and educational content include Acorns, E*TRADE, and Robinhood. Podcasts including interviews, analysis, and industry insights from successful investors and industry experts include "Invest Like the Best," "Motley Fool Money," and "The Investors Podcast." In order to accommodate a wide range of learning tastes and styles, video platforms such as YouTube offer an abundance of educational channels and lessons on topics such as stock market investing, technical analysis, and market trends.

To sum up, educational materials are essential for providing people and companies with the information and abilities to manage the stock market successfully. A vast range of resources and platforms are accessible to meet various learning needs and preferences, from online courses and classic books to seminars, financial news sources, simulation tools, and regulatory information. Through the use of these tools, investors can establish a solid knowledge base, create strategies that work, and make well-informed decisions that support their financial objectives. Success in the dynamic and always changing stock market world requires ongoing education and keeping abreast of market trends.

Analytical Tools

Analytical tools play a crucial role in the world of investing, providing investors with the means to evaluate investments, assess risks, and make informed decisions. These tools cover a broad spectrum of approaches and procedures intended to analyze economic indicators, market trends, and financial data. Investors can improve portfolio performance, reduce risk, and gain a better knowledge of investing opportunities by successfully utilizing analytical tools.

Fundamental analysis is one of the primary analytical methods used in investment analysis. To determine a company's intrinsic value, this method entails analyzing its financial statements, management team, competitive posture, and industry trends. To evaluate if a stock is cheap or expensive in relation to its market price, fundamental analysts look at important financial indicators, including earnings per share (EPS), profit margins, and return on equity (ROE). Other criteria include sales growth. Investors can find good companies with strong financial fundamentals and development potential by doing a thorough fundamental analysis. This allows investors to make well-informed investment decisions that are in line with their long-term goals.

Another popular analytical technique is technical analysis, which forecasts future price changes by examining past price and volume data. To spot patterns and trends in stock prices, technical analysts use graphs, charts, and technical indicators like MACD (Moving Average Convergence Divergence), RSI, and moving averages. Technical analysts strive to forecast price changes and pinpoint possible trade entry and exit opportunities by examining market patterns and momentum. Technical analysis complements fundamental analysis in the process of making investment decisions, even if its primary application is in short-term trading methods. It offers insightful information about investor behavior and market sentiment.

To successfully identify and mitigate investment risks, risk management tools are necessary. Among these tools are risk indicators that measure the degree of volatility and possible downside risk associated with investments, such as beta, standard deviation, and Value at Risk (VaR). A stock's sensitivity to market fluctuations is gauged by its beta value; a beta of more than one indicates higher volatility relative to the market, while a beta of less than one indicates lesser volatility. By calculating the dispersion of returns around the average return, the standard deviation can be used to determine how risky a portfolio is. Value at Risk, or VaR, is a tool used by investors to determine their risk tolerance and put effective risk management measures into practice. It calculates the highest possible loss under typical market conditions over a given time period.

Large datasets are analyzed and investing insights are obtained using quantitative analysis, which makes use of mathematical models, statistical methods, and computational algorithms. Based on past data and statistical probabilities, quantitative analysts, or quants, use quantitative models to forecast asset prices, optimize portfolio allocations, and pinpoint trading opportunities.

To produce investment signals and strategies, these models may take into account variables, including price changes, trade volumes, market trends, and economic data. By utilizing cutting-edge analytical methods and computational resources, quantitative analysis helps investors make data-driven decisions, improve portfolio diversity, and generate higher risk-adjusted returns.

Sentiment analysis is a technique that examines social media, news stories, and other public opinion sources to determine the sentiment of the market and investor sentiments. Sentiment analysts track changes in investor sentiment, sentiment scores, and sentiment indexes to identify movements in market sentiment and possible future trends. Analysts can spot market extremes, sentiment biases, and contrarian investment possibilities by analyzing investor sentiment. By offering insights into market psychology and emotion-driven price movements, sentiment analysis enhances other analytical techniques and helps investors predict market trends and modify their investing strategy accordingly.

Economic analysis evaluates the overall state of the economy and how it affects investments by looking at macroeconomic variables, including GDP growth, interest rates, inflation rates, and employment data. Economists examine economic indicators, governmental regulations, and geopolitical events to predict economic trends and their consequences for financial markets. Investment researchers can spot industries with development potential, predict shifts in consumer purchasing habits, and modify portfolio allocations in response to economic projections by including economic analysis into their study.

Scenario analysis and stress testing are two methods for evaluating an investment portfolio's resistance to varying market conditions and unfavorable circumstances. In scenario analysis, analysts model different financial, geopolitical, and economic situations in order to assess risk exposures and portfolio performance. Stress testing exposes portfolios to extreme market conditions—like precipitous drops in stock prices or recessions—to quantify possible losses and pinpoint weak points. Investors can reduce risks related to market volatility and unforeseen occurrences, optimize asset allocation, and strengthen portfolio resilience by performing scenario analysis and stress testing.

Analytical tools are essential for investors who want to understand the intricacies of financial markets and use them to guide their investing decisions. Investors can increase their chances of achieving their long-term financial goals and accumulating wealth by using a variety of analytical tools, such as economic analysis to understand macroeconomic trends, scenario analysis, and stress testing to improve portfolio resilience, technical analysis to identify market trends, quantitative analysis to leverage data-driven insights, risk management tools to assess and mitigate risks, and sentiment analysis to gauge market sentiment. To help investors pursue their financial objectives, each analytical tool offers a different viewpoint and insight into potential dangers and investment opportunities. This gives investors the ability to proceed with confidence and caution.

Staying Informed

For investors to navigate the complexities of financial markets, make astute choices, and adapt to evolving economic conditions, they must empower themselves with knowledge about the stock market. In today's interconnected global economy, this means knowing where to find timely and relevant information, tracking market trends, and interpreting economic indicators that impact portfolio performance and investment decisions.

Financial media and news sources are among the main resources for stock market information. These include reliable resources like the financial sections of well-known publications like The Wall Street Journal and Financial Times and CNBC, Bloomberg, and Reuters. These sources include in-depth reporting on corporate earnings releases, economic data releases, geopolitical occurrences that affect stock prices, and sentiment in the market as well as worldwide financial markets. These platforms provide investors with up-to-date breaking news, market trends, and expert analysis to help them make informed decisions and develop their investment strategy.

Digital platforms and financial websites are important sources of information for investors, in addition to traditional media. Websites like Yahoo Finance, Google Finance, and MarketWatch provide real-time stock quotes, interactive charts, and market research tools. These tools allow investors to track particular stocks, keep an eye on market moves, and access financial data from any location in the world. Users can create watchlists, get alerts when prices change, and obtain research reports and analysis from analysts and industry professionals with these platforms' customized capabilities.

Social media sites have become significant resources for stock market information. Financial professionals, analysts, and institutional investors, in particular, utilize Twitter extensively to disseminate real-time observations, market commentary, and breaking news. Subscribing to the accounts of financial gurus, investment firms, and industry influencers can provide investors with insights into market trends, corporate advancements, and investment opportunities. However, it's crucial to exercise caution and verify information from reliable sources, as social media can also propagate rumors and false information that could potentially influence investing decisions.

Investor relations websites and business earnings calls are additional sources of information for investors. Publicly listed corporations frequently hold earnings calls with analysts, investors, and the media to go over financial results, strategic objectives, and future outlooks. These conversations offer insightful information about a business's success, potential for expansion, and management's evaluation of the state of the market. Financial statements, annual reports, and corporate presentations that provide comprehensive details on business operations, market strategy, and key performance metrics necessary for assessing investment prospects are accessible on companies' investor relations websites.

To stay up to date on market trends and investment opportunities, financial institutions and brokerage firms provide research reports and educational tools. Comprehensive study of market trends, company-specific factors, and industry sectors influencing stock prices and investment decisions may be found in analyst reports, market research publications, and industry insights. Using these tools, investors can evaluate value indicators, carry out fundamental research, and find possible investments that fit their risk tolerance and investing objectives.

Through investing clubs, forums, and conferences, one can foster a sense of community and interact with peers and professionals in the financial sector. This not only allows for the sharing of experiences and insights into market trends but also encourages the exchange of ideas about investment methods. Investment clubs provide a platform for members with diverse backgrounds and levels of experience to engage in cooperative learning, stock research, and portfolio management discussions. Keynote addresses, panel discussions, and networking opportunities at conferences and industry events further enhance this sense of community, providing attendees with the opportunity to engage with peers, industry experts, and thought leaders and gain valuable insights into new trends and best practices in stock market trading.

Finally, important information sources for investors to be updated about the stock market include regulatory filings and economic data. The Securities and Exchange Commission (SEC) receives regulatory filings, such as quarterly reports (10-Q) and annual reports (10-K), which offer comprehensive financial disclosures and valuable insights into a company's operations, risks, and financial performance. Economic indicators provide macroeconomic insights that affect investor confidence, interest rates, and market sentiment, which in turn affects stock prices and market trends. Examples of these indicators include GDP, unemployment rates, and inflation data.

To sum up, in order to remain informed about the stock market, one must constantly keep an eye on financial news, make use of digital and social media channels, access company disclosures and analyst reports, take advantage of educational opportunities, connect with professionals in the field, and keep an eye on economic indicators. In an ever-changing global financial market, investors can improve their capacity to make well-informed decisions, manage portfolio risks, and achieve long-term financial success by remaining informed through a variety of sources and adhering to a disciplined approach to research and analysis.

CHAPTER X

Putting It All Together

Developing Your Investment Plan

Creating an investing plan is critical to reaching long-term financial objectives and wealth accumulation. A well-written investment plan acts as a road map describing your goals for your finances, risk tolerance, investment techniques, and when you want to reach them. Whether you're new to investing or have experience in the financial markets, making a structured investment plan gives you focus, discipline, and a methodical way to manage your money.

Clearly defining your financial objectives is the first step in creating an investment strategy. These objectives differ greatly from person to person and can include retirement savings, paying for college, buying a house, or creating a safety net for one's finances. You may create a framework for deciding how much to invest, where to put your money, and when to accomplish each goal by setting clear priorities for each one. Setting attainable, quantifiable, and time-bound goals will help your investment strategy stay on course.

Understanding your risk tolerance is a crucial aspect of developing an investment strategy. It's the measure of your ability and willingness to withstand fluctuations in the value of your investments over the long term. Your risk tolerance is influenced by factors such as age, income stability, financial expertise, and personal preferences. Conservative investors may prefer low-risk investments with stable returns, while risk-tolerant investors may be more comfortable with volatile assets that could potentially yield higher returns. By determining your risk tolerance, you can select investments that align with your financial goals and comfort level, thereby guiding your decision-making process.

Asset allocation, a key strategy in investment planning, involves dividing your portfolio among various asset classes such as stocks, bonds, cash equivalents, and alternative assets. The aim of asset allocation is to diversify your investments across different asset classes that respond to market conditions, thereby potentially maximizing returns while managing risk. By capitalizing on opportunities in a variety of industries and asset classes, a diversified portfolio can enhance long-term performance and mitigate the impact of market volatility.

Choosing particular assets becomes clear once your risk tolerance, asset allocation plan, and financial objectives have been established. In order to assess whether individual securities, mutual funds, exchange-traded funds (ETFs), or other investment vehicles match your investing objectives and risk tolerance, you must undertake research and due diligence. Historical performance, management experience, costs and fees, liquidity, and tax ramifications are all important factors to take into account. Diversification within each asset class is crucial in order to distribute risk and seize opportunities in various market segments.

Regular and thorough portfolio monitoring and review are vital components of a successful investment plan. The performance of your investments can be influenced by rapid changes in economic conditions and the dynamic nature of financial markets. Monitoring involves tracking the performance of each security and your overall portfolio in relation to your financial goals and industry standards. Regular reviews provide an opportunity to reassess your investment approach, rebalance your portfolio as necessary, and make adjustments in response to changing market conditions, personal circumstances, or investment objectives. By staying vigilant and proactive, you can ensure your investment plan remains aligned with your goals and market trends.

Planning for investments must also take taxes into account. Tax payments can be reduced and after-tax earnings can be increased by being aware of the tax consequences of your assets. The tax efficiency of your investment portfolio can be improved by employing techniques like tax-efficient asset allocation, tax-loss harvesting, and making use of tax-advantaged funds like 401(k)s and IRAs. For advice on maximizing your investment strategy to attain tax-efficient results in line with your financial objectives, speak with a tax expert or financial counselor.

Developing a long-term outlook for your investments is essential to attaining steady growth and enduring market swings. Through long-term investment, you may focus on reaching your financial objectives over a prolonged period of time while navigating short-term market turbulence and taking advantage of compounding gains. Through consistent and intelligent investment selections, you position yourself for long-term success and wealth building by upholding discipline, sticking to your plan, and avoiding emotional reactions to market changes.

Last but not least, keeping your investment strategy up to date and in line with your changing financial objectives, personal circumstances, and market conditions requires regular reviews and revisions. A change in job, marriage, having children, or approaching retirement may require you to make changes to your asset allocation and investing strategy. You can increase your chances of long-term financial security and prosperity by being proactive and flexible in order to adjust your investment plan to market possibilities, shifting goals, and economic trends.

Creating an investment plan necessitates carefully taking into account your long-term goals, tax consequences, asset allocation strategy, risk tolerance, and investment selection criteria. You provide yourself the ability to make well-informed decisions, maximize portfolio performance, and clearly and confidently accomplish your financial goals in a constantly changing and dynamic financial environment by using a systematic and disciplined approach to investing management.

Common Mistakes to Avoid

The world of investing can be both thrilling and intimidating; it is a total of chances for financial gain and hazards that could prevent you from achieving your objectives. Building a sound investing strategy and obtaining long-term financial security requires understanding frequent mistakes made by investors and knowing how to avoid them.

A prevalent error investors commit is the need for well-defined financial goals and objectives. Investors may design their portfolios haphazardly and miss out on chances that align with their long-term aims if they lack direction and clarity in their decisions. Investors can establish a roadmap for investments by setting specific, quantifiable, and realistic financial goals. These goals also serve as a framework for assessing performance over time and help guide decisions about asset allocation.

Not diversifying enough is another crucial error. Investors are exposed to increased risk and volatility when they concentrate their assets on a single stock, industry, or asset class. Spreading assets over several asset classes, sectors, geographical areas, and security helps mitigate the negative effects of unforeseen circumstances on portfolio performance. Effective diversification can help investors minimize losses during market downturns and seize growth opportunities across a range of market circumstances.

Emotional decision-making is a frequent trap that can sabotage long-term financial objectives by encouraging rash investment decisions. Suboptimal investing outcomes can arise from emotional responses to market volatility, such as panic selling during market downturns or chasing hot investment trends during market euphoria. Rather than acting rashly in response to transient market swings, disciplined and logical investors base their judgments on careful investigation, analysis, and adherence to their investing strategy.

Due to transaction fees, taxes, and the possibility of underperforming the market, overtrading and frequent portfolio turnover could be better for the performance of investments. Excessive trading by investors can result in increased costs and fees, which lowers portfolio returns overall. Alternatively, investors can reduce the impact of trading expenses on portfolio performance and take advantage of compounding returns by implementing a buy-and-hold strategy that is in line with long-term investment objectives.

Another big mistake that investors frequently make is to ignore the basics of risk management. Inadequate evaluation and management of investment risks can subject portfolios to unwarranted volatility and possible losses. Identifying risks, such as credit, market, and liquidity concerns, and putting policies in place to diversify, hedge, or lessen exposure to these risks are all necessary for effective risk management. Investing strategies that include risk management strategies help investors safeguard capital and maintain wealth over time.

One typical mistake that can cause investment portfolios to drift and deviate from planned asset allocation targets is the failure to assess and rebalance them on a regular basis. Asset classes may perform differently due to market and economic movements, which could vary the portfolio's risk-return profile. Through periodic portfolio reviews, investors can evaluate performance, adjust asset allocations, and realign investments with their long-term goals and risk tolerance. They are rebalancing guarantees that the portfolio stays risk-adjusted, diversified, and optimized for reaching financial objectives.

Speculative approaches that can jeopardize the success of an investment include chasing performance or trying to time the market. Those who invest in assets that have recently outperformed in an attempt to emulate prior performance risk missing out on growth prospects in undervalued or underperforming industries. In a similar vein, trying to timing the market by forecasting brief price changes frequently leads to lost chances and higher transaction expenses. Adhering to their investing strategy, focusing on long-term trends, and resisting the temptation of market timing or performance chasing are characteristics of successful investors.

Investors may find it more difficult to evaluate investment opportunities and make well-informed selections if they lack study and understanding about investing. To assess the possible risks and returns of investments, one must have a basic understanding of topics such as financial statements, valuation measurements, and economic indicators. Using analytical tools, staying up to date on market trends, and conducting in-depth research enable investors to make well-informed investment decisions that are compatible with their risk tolerance and financial objectives.

Ignoring the effect of taxes, fees, and expenses on investment returns is another typical error that, can degrade portfolio performance over time. Excessive costs related to managed accounts, mutual funds, and ETFs can drastically lower net returns, particularly when accumulated over an extended period of time. Likewise, disregarding the tax consequences of investment choices may lead to increased tax obligations and reduced post-tax gains. Tax-efficient investing methods should be investigated, investment costs should be kept to a minimum, and portfolio returns should be maximized overall.

Last but not least, neglecting to obtain expert counsel when necessary, might deny investors access to priceless knowledge, tactics, and insights. Investment experts and financial consultants can offer individualized advice based on an investor's risk tolerance, life goals, and financial objectives. In times of market turbulence, having a trustworthy advisor by your side can help you manage difficult financial choices, maximize portfolio performance, and maintain discipline.

In summary, avoiding typical investment blunders necessitates self-control, vigilance, and a methodical approach to asset management. Long-term financial performance can be improved for investors by setting clear financial objectives, diversifying wisely, avoiding rash decisions, managing risk sensibly, and performing extensive research. To successfully navigate the complexity of financial markets and accumulate wealth over time, one must maintain a disciplined investing plan, analyze portfolio performance on a regular basis, and seek professional assistance when necessary.

The Road Ahead

Stock investing is a journey that gives people the chance to safeguard their future, accumulate money, and meet their financial objectives. A few crucial factors and actions can help investors make wise choices and successfully negotiate the financial markets' intricacies as they embark on their journey.

It's crucial to start by comprehending the foundational ideas of stock investing. Investing in stocks gives investors a piece of ownership in publicly listed corporations as well as the possibility of capital gains and dividend payments. When buying stocks, one must analyze a company's financial standing, future growth potential, market trends, and risk management strategies to maximize returns on investment.

Setting definite financial objectives is one of the first stages towards stock investing. When investors set specific goals, such as supporting their school, saving for retirement, or reaching other milestones, their investing strategy can be adjusted appropriately. Investors can create a roadmap that directs asset allocation decisions and guarantees their investments are by their long-term objectives by establishing quantifiable targets with realistic timeframes.

In order to have a diverse investment portfolio, asset allocation is essential. Spreading assets over several asset classes, sectors, and geographical areas lowers risk and improves the robustness of a portfolio as a whole. Adequate diversification helps investors minimize the effects of market volatility and seize expansion opportunities across a range of industries and market circumstances. Strategic asset allocation promotes a balanced wealth-building and preservation approach by matching investors' time horizons, financial goals, and risk tolerance.

Another crucial component of navigating the stock investment path is risk management. Over time, protecting money and preserving wealth is aided by evaluating and reducing investment risks such as credit, market, and liquidity risks. Investors can protect themselves from possible losses and efficiently navigate financial market volatility by putting risk management tactics like diversification, asset allocation rebalancing, and stop-loss orders into practice.

Making educated financial selections requires familiarity with economic trends, market dynamics, and investing concepts. Continual education and keeping abreast of macroeconomic events, industry advancements, and regulatory changes enable investors to assess opportunities, predict market trends, and modify their investment strategy accordingly. Access to instructional materials, seminars, and speaking with financial consultants helps people become more knowledgeable and confident about managing their investment portfolios.

Achieving financial success requires developing and sticking to a disciplined investing strategy over an extended period of time. Setting investment guidelines, keeping a diversified portfolio, tracking results often, and adjusting according to changing market conditions and individual financial objectives are all part of a disciplined strategy. Investors can achieve their long-term goals while navigating obstacles and seizing opportunities by maintaining discipline and avoiding emotional responses to market swings.

Gaining a solid foundation in finance and comprehension of investment principles enables investors to negotiate the intricacies of stock market investing confidently. Fundamental analysis is a process that identifies investment opportunities with great potential for creating long-term value by analyzing business financials, industry trends, competitive positioning, and growth possibilities. In contrast, technical analysis forecasts future price movements and helps traders make well-informed decisions by using previous price data and market indications.

A dividend's ability to increase overall return on investments and produce passive income should also be taken into account by investors. Dividend-paying stocks appeal to income-oriented investors looking for stability and growth in their portfolios since they offer consistent income streams and the possibility of capital appreciation. Dividends can be reinvested through dividend reinvestment plans (DRIPs) or transferred to other investments to expedite wealth accumulation.

Portfolio performance monitoring and routine reviews are crucial to maximizing investment returns and keeping on course to meet financial objectives. Through monitoring asset allocation, examining investment results, and evaluating portfolio diversification, investors can discern the window of opportunity for rebalancing and necessary modifications to their investment plans. Frequent reviews also help investors analyze risk-adjusted returns, compare performance to benchmarks, and make well-informed decisions based on the state of the market and the economy.

Staying flexible and sensitive to shifting market conditions and economic landscapes is crucial for investors navigating the stock market's future. Market cycles, geopolitical developments, and industrial upheavals can affect the performance of investments and necessitate modifying portfolio strategy. Building resilience and attaining long-term financial success are facilitated by keeping an open mind regarding market events, adopting a flexible approach to investing, and getting expert advice when necessary.

The path toward stock investment presents chances for generating money, attaining financial autonomy, and realizing individual financial objectives. Investors can effectively traverse the complexities of financial markets by comprehending basic investing principles, defining clear goals, diversifying portfolios, controlling risks, continuing education, and adhering to a disciplined investment approach. Investing methods, portfolio diversification, and performance monitoring allow investors to take advantage of opportunities, reduce risk, and achieve long-term sustainable gain. Starting a stock investing journey involves perseverance, hard work, and a dedication to financial planning that enables people to create a safe and wealthy future by making a wise investment choice.

CONCLUSION

Stock Market Starter: A Beginner's Guide to Investing: Building Wealth One Share at a Time" is an essential resource for novice investors embarking on their journey in the stock market. With the help of this thorough book, readers will get the necessary knowledge, valuable tactics, and insightful understanding needed to navigate the difficulties of investing confidently.

Key ideas such as comprehending stocks, the workings of the stock market, vocabulary related to the stock market, establishing financial objectives, constructing diverse investment portfolios, and evaluating business success are all introduced to readers throughout the book. The handbook strongly emphasizes the value of risk management techniques, disciplined investing methods, and market trend awareness.

This book gives readers the confidence to make well-informed decisions that align with their risk tolerance and financial objectives by demystifying the complexities of stock market investment. It promotes proactively accumulating wealth through wise investing techniques, lifelong learning, and adaptation to market conditions.

"Stock Market Starter" offers the fundamental information and valuable tools required to start a successful investing journey, regardless of the readers' goals—saving for retirement, financing education, or reaching other financial milestones. Focusing on methodically accumulating money, one share at a time, this book gives novices the self-assurance and know-how to successfully navigate the stock market and achieve their financial goals with direction and clarity.

Thank you for buying and reading/ listening to our book. If you found this book useful/ helpful please take a few minutes and leave a review on the platform where you purchased our book. Your feedback matters greatly to us.

www.ingramcontent.com/pod-product-compliance
Lightning Source LLC
Chambersburg PA
CBHW072009150726
47999CB00002B/575